ENTREPRENEUR HACKS: A COLLECTION OF STRANGE, BIZARRE AND INGENIOUS ONLINE AND OFFLINE BUSINESS HACKS

BY

JACK KOGERA

DEDICATION

This book is dedicated to my darling wife, Veronica and our 2 children. Without you, my dreams are incomplete. I thank you from the bottom of my heart for the sacrifices you have made, faith in me, believing in me, standing by me and encouraging me when things fell apart.

To my parents, Josephat and Peninah Kogera thank you for the values you instilled in me. And for being selfless with your resources, time and love. To my sisters Aileen, Flora and Fiona thanks for loving me and being there for me.

To all the dreamers who at some point lost hope in their dreams, it is never too late to put the pieces together and pursue your dream. Visit my website http://mulazz.com for tons of free trainings, videos and ebooks on online business success and personal development.

More Books By Jack Kogera. Get your copy of any one of these from Amazon.com today!

(a) **Niche Selection Simplified** – Learn 13 proven steps to selecting a profitable niche

(b) **Content Machine:** Why The Old Way of Article Marketing Does Not Work And How To Succeed With it Now

(c) **Steve Jobs:** 7 Killer Online Marketing Success Strategies That We Learn From Steve Jobs *(***This book is in the Top 100 free books in Kindle Store. Download it today for free***)*.

(d) **DOTCOM SECRETS:** 33 Things I Would Have Paid Good Money to Know Before I Started In Online Marketing

(e) Jab, Jab, Jab Knockout: How To Compete In A Saturated Niche Market And Make Money Online

(f) **9 Online Marketing Success Strategies** That We Learn From Sam Walton (Walmart Founder). *Includes Bonus Chapter on 3 Proven Ways To Make Money Online In The Next 24 hours*

Table of Contents

Introduction

I want to thank you for purchasing this book. This book is a collection of some of the most bizarre, ingenious but effective hacks that will both inspire and amuse you. Hacking has become commonplace in our modern day culture because it is a quick procedure or way of doing something to achieve results quickly. Hacking is:

(a) Ingenious

(b) Solves a problem

(c) Not a well-known solution or straight forward solution to a problem. But an effective solution nonetheless.

For Entrepreneurs, business hacks save time, increase efficiency and where applicable make you money faster. Additionally, in this book you will learn proven step by step strategies that you can easily implement in your online or offline business. This book is a pleasurable and valuable read that you will come back to often.

1. Marketing Hacks

Be Weird

There is a school of thought that says that when you are choosing a niche, find something small and highly targeted. This is great if you end up being the big fish in a little pond. But if another big fish comes along in that same pond – or worse yet, a whole damned school of big fish – then you're in trouble.

So here's a thought – why not be a little fish in a big pond, but do it in such a way that you stand out like a neon red fish in a school of gray boring fish? Let's say you want to write a marketing blog – guess what? There are a million marketing blogs (or more) and the field is darn crowded. That's the bad news. The good news is there are plenty of people who want to read about marketing every day – you just have to stand out of the crowd so they can find you.

So maybe instead of your niche being, "Great Marketing Ideas!" Or "Super Swell Marketing Tips!" your niche could be, "Marketing for Chiropractors Who Hate Marketing." Or perhaps, "Marketing For Cookbook Authors." See what's happening? You're in a HUGE niche, but you've carved it down to a very specific group within that niche. Now that's good, but it's still not great. After all, they're likely to visit you, but will they remember you? Will they race to open your email each time you send them something? Maybe. Maybe not. So what we need to do is kick it up another notch.

And this is where you get weird, my friend. Don't worry – secretly we are ALL weird. Being "weird" simply means being "different" than the crowd. And online, that's a really, really good thing. Mind you, this advice goes for websites and products as well as blogs. Take this one for example...

http://bit.ly/selleckwater

This website is exclusively dedicated to 3 things: Tom Selleck, Waterfalls and Sandwiches. You'll be surprised at all the different ways those 3 things can come together. HA! Okay, I admit, I was having a little fun with you there. While that is an actual website, it's best used as an illustration of perhaps taking "weird" just a bit too far.

We simply want to go one step further to make our brand sticky in the minds of our visitors. You can do that with a memorable URL, such as EatMyFrog.com. Seriously, are you likely to forget "Eat My Frog dot com?" Not likely. Another technique to set you apart and make yourself memorable is by adding some personality to your name. And it's easy to do – just give yourself a nickname. Is this weird? I hope so – after all, that is what we're going for. Remember, "Weird" = memorable.

Here are ideas for nicknames – take something about yourself, be it a past profession, a hobby, a physical feature, a personality quirk or whatever, and give yourself a name centered around that. Some examples:

Farming could be "Farm Girl"

Truck driving - "The Mad Truck Driver"

Ex Military – "Soldier Sue" or "Sailor Sam."

Physical features - "The Redhead"

Hobbies - "Ski Fanatic"

Foods You Love - "Tony Bagels"

Better still, nickname yourself after your Expertise. For example:

Mr. Googlehead for an SEO expert. Now when they get an email from "The Redhead" or "Mr. Googlehead," they're going to remember you, which means they are much more likely to open and read your email. Now not only is your niche properly carved down to make you an important little fish in a big pond – you're also a more MEMORABLE fish. Think it's silly? It's simply good marketing sense. You're branding yourself to make yourself memorable – and memorable is good!

Make Money No Matter WHO Your Customers Buy From
Let's say you sell a high ticket software solution to businesses. You drive traffic to your website and then try to convince those visitors that your product is better than all the others, thus converting them into sales. But what if you took a slightly different tact?

First, you sign up as an affiliate with all of your competitors. Next, you write a report in which you feature ALL of the software solutions, not just yours. Of course you feature yours first, but you also fairly cover all of your competitors' products and provide links to their websites.

Result? First, you come across as an unbiased, helpful expert instead of a sales person. Second, you likely make more sales of your own product. Third, you get paid even when customers decide to purchase from your competitors. And fourth, you're building a list you can continue to market to for a long time to come.

4

This might even work in some offline niches as well, such as swimming pool sales and installation. If competitors don't have an affiliate program, approach them to set one up.

Just imagine going to an offline client and telling them they can make money even when a customer goes with their competitor – what a great way to get in the door and get them listening to what you have to say.

Doing The Opposite in Coffee Marketing

The big coffee chains are trying to run your little mom and pop coffee shop out of business – what do you do? You could try to compete on their terms, but you'll likely lose. Or you could do the unexpected and get free press to boot. So what's the opposite of being loyal to, say, Starbucks? It's being disloyal. Six Washington DC coffee shops have banded together to offer a disloyalty card to encourage customers to visit different neighborhoods and try different coffees from each shop.

Two great ideas are found here: The first of course is to watch what everyone else is doing and then do the opposite. Loyalty programs abound, so why not start a disloyalty program? It's catchy and newsworthy, garnering free publicity just for printing up and distributing some "disloyalty cards." And the second lesson is to band together with your competition to create a bigger, stronger team that can offer more to your customers.

Marijuana Smuggler Seeks Job

Here's another startling example of doing the opposite to promote your brand: Brian O'dea posted the following ad when looking for work:

Employment Wanted -Former Marijuana Smuggler

Having successfully completed a ten year sentence, incident-free, for importing 75 tons of marijuana into the United States. I am now seeking a legal and legitimate means to support myself and my family.

Business Experience - Owned and operated a successful fishing business - multi-vessel, one airplane, one island and processing facility. Simultaneously owned and operated a fleet of tractor-trailer trucks conducting business in the western United States. During this time I also co-owned and participated in the executive level management of 120 people worldwide in a successful pot smuggling venture with revenues in excess of US$100 million annually. I took responsibility for my own actions, and received a ten year sentence in the United States while others walked free for their cooperation.

Attributes - I am an expert in all levels of security; I have extensive computer skills, am personable, outgoing, well-educated, reliable, clean and sober. I have spoken in schools to thousands of kids and parent groups over the past ten years on "the consequences of choice", and received public recognition from the RCMP for community service. I am well-traveled and speak English, French and Spanish. References available from friends, family, the U.S. District Attorney, etc.

While most people with Brian's background would have downplayed his past in the hopes that someone would hire him anyway, Brian followed his gut instinct, did the opposite and revealed all in a public advertisement in a major newspaper. Result? Plenty of free media coverage and an amazing 600 responses.

So go ahead – turn your negatives into positives - and do what you think is right – not what everyone else says you should do, or what "conventional wisdom" advises. Sometimes taking what we believe is the correct course of action goes against the grain and seems to be the opposite of what the world expects. So what? If it means being true to yourself, there's an excellent chance you and your business will fare far better for having taken the leap of faith than if you'd taken the common road.

As to doing the opposite of what people expect, the character George on Seinfeld did this for an entire episode, and for perhaps the first time ever, things worked out brilliantly for him.

True, you're not a TV character – but the fact is you've only got one life. Do you want to live it as a copy of someone else's life, or do you want to stand apart from the crowd and be your own person?

Every great innovation began with people saying it either couldn't be done or it would never work. Forget the naysayers and dare to be different.

By the way – this is not new news – in fact it was almost a decade ago that this ad appeared, yet Brian is still banking off of this with his own website called, "HIGH – Confessions of an International Drug Smuggler."

http://www.brianodea.com/

UGLY Models

In our quest for success, we often imitate others who are already successful, hoping to duplicate what they've already done. And while modeling others is indeed an excellent success tactic, it results in numerous people in the same niche all doing the same things with very little differentiation. Obviously it's difficult to attract attention or customers when you're looking like and acting like everyone else – so why not do the opposite?

There is a modeling agency in the U.K. that has been doing exactly that for the past 40 years. While every other agency is looking for super young, super thin and super beautiful models, The Ugly Modeling Agency specializes in, umm, shall we say, "not so pretty" models?

To get the full effect you'll want to watch the video...http://bit.ly/uglymodels

Which leads to the obvious question – what can you do in your business that is the OPPOSITE of what everyone else has been doing? As this video demonstrates, nothing should be considered too radical, and it's the most bizarre which might pay off the most.

Take a good look at each facet of your business, at your relationship to your customers and at your products and services. Now ask yourself – what can you do 180 degrees differently? How can you stand so far away from the pack, that you no longer have any competition?

Don't be too quick to discount the answers you receive. No doubt the founder of this modeling agency thought his idea was crazy – yet it's been working for 4 decades.

The Time I Was Questioned by Police For Knitting in Starbucks. How do you get a mundane story to carry on a life of its own and get picked up by numerous websites including big ones like The Huffington Post? By finding the right angle to present the story. As you know a great story written in a boring manner isn't as likely to be shared as a mundane story written with an exciting slant to it – something Gregory Patrick seems to know well.

Gregory knits. In fact, he has his own knitting blog. And when he wrote his post about knitting in Starbucks and being questioned by the police, it quickly went viral. Seriously, how can you read, "The Time I Was Questioned by Police for Knitting in Starbucks" and not continue reading? The thought that no doubt immediately entered the minds of most readers is that the police were hassling someone just because they were knitting in a coffee shop. What's the big deal? People surf the Internet in coffee shops, they write, they read, they do all manner of things – why not knit? Is there a posse of anti-knitting cops out there? Or did Starbucks call the cops on this person because they thought he was knitting a bomb?

Turns out the cops were simply debating among themselves whether this guy was doing needlepoint or knitting. But to find this out, you've got to read well into the story and by that time you're hooked anyway. Had Gregory simply used a title like, "Cops confused about knitting," or "Here's the difference between needlepoint and knitting" it's doubtful the story would have gone viral.

Gregory sold all of his knitted teddy bears within minutes of the story being picked up by other websites. It's a shame he only had a few to sell, since he probably could have sold far, far more.

http://gregorypatrick.bigcartel.com/

So the next time you're about to write a blogpost, think about this – how can you present the information in a way that will compel people to go read it, and maybe even forward it to their friends or post a link to it on their website?

Traveling The World Via Customers' Couches
David Menasche loved his work as a high school English teacher. He loved his subject and was even more passionate about helping his

students. Then he was diagnosed with brain cancer, which ultimately affected David's vision, memory, mobility – and his ability to continue teaching.

This is where most people would give up and go home to live out their remaining days, but not David. He decided he wanted to visit as many of his students as possible to see first-hand how they were fairing in life. And so he made a post on Facebook, asking if any of his students had a couch he could sleep on. Within 48 hours of posting, former students in more than fifty cities replied with offers of support and shelter.

Traveling more than 8,000 miles from Miami to New York to San Francisco, David visited hundreds of his former students and wrote a book about his experience, called "The Priority List." Now then, here's my crazy (or perhaps not so crazy) idea: If you have a loyal following in your niche, what if you followed David's example? What if you decided you wanted to see your country, or perhaps another country, and you ask your followers if they have a couch you can borrow for a night?

Imagine meeting many of your best customers face to face for the first time. Imagine the relationships you could foster and the places you could see! A blogger might travel the world this way and write about their adventures. In fact, I know there are already several bloggers doing this exact thing. Their expenses are low because they stay with their readers, and they write a post or two about each stop along the way.

If you have the travel bug, this might be something you should explore further. If your blog is profitable, you can get paid for traveling the world and making memories that will last a life time.

Guy Quits Job to Play Starcraft 2: Clears $5,000 a month!
Steven Bonnell didn't want to clean carpets anymore – he just wanted to stay home and play his favorite video game, Starcraft 2. He ended up earning $5,000 a month playing the game and yet he was not even the best in the world. In fact, he didn't even play in the Starcraft tournaments. How did Steven end up earning a living doing the thing that he loves the most? He simply played the game and streamed it live via Justin.tv, and then he placed the videos on YouTube. Because he was highly animated on the videos, he attracted a very loyal following, earning about $3500 a month in ad revenue. Plus, he taught others how to play. This brought him an additional $1500 a month.

Lessons learned

1. If you can think just a little bit creatively, you can probably find a way to earn your living doing the thing you love the most.
2. You don't have to be the best of the best – you just need some sort of edge. In Steven's case, he was highly entertaining and passionate and it came through on his

videos.

3. Video games are a HUGE market full of rabid fans, so if this is your niches, there's plenty of money to be made.

4. Live streaming combined with placing the highlights on YouTube is a great marketing combination.

5. It's okay not to be perfect. If you're waiting until you're an expert or the best of the best to launch your business or share yourself with the world, you'll never be ready. Just get out there and start marketing what you do have – and see what happens.

6. If a guy can earn $60,000 playing a video game, what CAN'T you do??

PS: Thanks for reading thus far. I very much value your time and input. Please leave a review for this book in Amazon.

Do This To Double Your Sales

Offer a trial period or a free sample. Whatever your product or service is, offer a $1 seven day trial, or a free chapter or video, or SOMETHING to prove you deserve your customer's money.

The reason is two-fold:

First, you will inspire a great deal of confidence in your prospect. If you're offering the $1 trial, you remove the buyer's resistance. Who isn't willing to risk a buck to try something they really want? If you're offering a free sample such as the chapter or video, you are PROVING that you deliver before they ever buy.

Second, if your product or service is excellent and it delivers on what it promises, you will increase your sales dramatically. Often a low cost trial can double and even triple your conversions. And if executed correctly a free sample can put your customer on the edge of their seat, wanting the rest of the information.

HINT: End your free chapter or free video with plenty of teasers of what's to come in the rest of the material.

If you are not giving your prospects a free or inexpensive way to sample your products, you are losing sales.

Borrowing a Page From Groupon for your Business
No doubt you're heard of Groupon: That's the site that offers a special deal each day, but only IF enough people say they want the deal. And there are other group buying sites, too, such as LivingSocial. Even Facebook and The New York Times have jumped on the group buying bandwagon.

So how can this help your business? Here are 3 ideas you can implement immediately...

1. Ask your customers which products you should develop. This can be as easy as using a like button or taking a survey. Let them know that the most popular choice(s) will be created and offered.
2. Ask which of your current or previous products your customers would like to see offered at a discount. The

winning product is placed on sale for 72 hours.

3. Create scarcity. Suggest a new product you want to develop,
    but let your customers know it is ONLY available to those
    who put up their hands and show their desire, and then it's
    only available to the first "X" number who ask for it. As soon
    as you hit that mark, close your offer and bill your customers.
    If any customer changes his or her mind and doesn't
    consummate the sale, simply open it back up for a few
    minutes until those remaining slots are filled.

You are not only gauging interest with this last one, you are also
creating scarcity. Plus you're getting paid up front for a product you
have not yet created.

NOTE: Be sure to create the product as quickly as possible, taking
no more than 14 days to do so. Let your buyers know when they can
expect delivery, and then make or beat the deadline.

Bottom line? Group buying is a great way to increase both customer
interaction and sales.

Don't Blindly Imitate the Guru

Just a quick thought – you see a guru using a particular service,
doing a particular technique, sending out a certain email, etc. And
you think, "Hey! If he's doing it, then it must be the thing to do,
right?" Well, not necessarily. Guru types make mistakes too. And
because they are generally playing in a bigger arena, they sometimes
make very big mistakes they quickly regret. The problem is, if you're

watching them then you can't know for certain if what they just did was a good idea or the stupidest idea ever.

On top of that, you don't know what their goals are. Maybe they're selling a $2 ebook because they're upselling a $97 course on the backend. So you sell a $2 ebook with no backend and then you wonder why you only made 6 sales – it could be because you're not a guru and so no one recognized your name and no one believed there could be value in something that costs $2.

That's why you should never blindly imitate a guru – you don't have the full story of what he/she is doing and whether or not it's working. However, if you see him repeatedly doing something which he could easily change, then you might want to jump in and try it yourself. For example, you see a guru continually sending out emails with the same strange subject line. Try it. If it wasn't working for him, he wouldn't keep doing it. Or at least we HOPE he wouldn't – he might have someone in a faraway office sending those emails for him and he doesn't even know the results.

Be cautious with imitating anyone, even the big dogs of marketing.

Bacon Salt
Two tech guys with zero food experience and no marketing budget what-so-ever launch a product called Bacon Salt. They look for people on social networks who love bacon and follow and friend them. A tiny percentage of those people get enthusiastic about Bacon

Salt and tell others. What starts as a handful of followers multiplies into 37,000 fans.

They begin getting press – first newspaper articles, then TV appearances, and eventually an appearance on Oprah. Two guys who knew nothing about the food industry and had no marketing budget now have a hit on their hands. They go on to create several other bacon flavored products which are now found in restaurants and grocery stores all over the world.

And their success started with a very small group of people on a social network. You too can do this same technique and succeed with your product.

http://www.baconsalt.com/

Why Introverts Make the Best Marketers
First of all, let me clarify that introverts aren't necessarily shy. They are, however, quieter than extroverts. Introverts talk plenty when they have something important to say, but they tend to stay quiet when the topic is small talk. Why? Because small talk isn't important to them.

Now then, let's say you have 2 salespeople - an extrovert and an introvert. The extrovert is likely to talk, talk and talk – which is exactly what you expect from a sales person. And in the midst of all this talking, the extrovert will make sales. But the introvert will do something the extrovert commonly fails to do – the introvert will ask questions and LISTEN to the answers.

I don't mean they wait for the prospect to stop talking so they can begin extolling all the many benefits of the product. I mean they listen. They want to know what's keeping the prospect awake at night in relation to the problem the product solves. They want to know the prospect's fears, desires, dreams, etc. They want to know what's worked for the prospect, what's failed for the prospect, and what that prospect really, truly wants so they can help this prospect get it.

And this same sales person will continue to use questions as they present their product or service, questions that direct the prospect to the desired conclusion - that this product is what they want and need. Everything else being equal, 9 times out of 10 the introvert salesperson will outsell the extrovert – all because they asked questions and listened closely to the answers.

Introverted marketers have the same advantage as extroverted sales people. They dig to discover what it is their prospects truly want. They ask questions, be it in person, over Skype, in forums, via email, etc. And they pay close attention to the answers. These same marketers spend time researching what successful marketers are doing. They don't assume they already have the answers – instead, they look to those who've succeeded and they ask how it was done and how it can be duplicated.

Now mind you, extroverts can master the skills of asking questions and listening to the answers as well as any introvert, if they try. It doesn't come as naturally for them, but it will come with practice. And if you look at the most successful people in the world, what you will find is they stand on the shoulders of those who came before. They asked questions, got the answers and used this knowledge to carve their place in the world. Try it. Next time someone asks you for advice, ask them questions first. Next time someone asks about your product, ask them about their needs first. Next time someone is on a forum looking for help, ask them for more information. And then pay close attention to what they say before you make your reply. It's an almost unknown fact that asking the right questions and listening to the answers can be one of the highest paying skills in the world.

Keeping Your Brain Happy

Keeping your brain happy will enable you to accomplish your tasks and see your intentions through. We all know what it's like to try to work when our brain is in a fog or just doesn't want to cooperate with us. We feel like we can't get it in gear, like everything takes too long and the end result is sadly lacking. Just like any other part of the body, brains can get tired. Suffering from cerebral fatigue results in a lack of new ideas, poor thinking, lousy problem solving and can even be a cause of depression.

Here then are 12 tips to keep your brain refreshed, energized and happy:

1) Mix it up. It's just common sense that if you spend hour after hour on the same task, you're going to get burnt out. So instead of writing articles for 8 hours straight, try writing articles for 2 hours, researching your next product for an hour, returning emails for an hour, etc.

2) Don't multi-task important stuff. Sure, you can listen to the radio while you're doing the dishes, but that's because neither one requires your full attention. When doing something important like learning a new skill from a webinar or working on your next product, don't be checking email or the score of the game. By not multi-tasking you'll accomplish more in less time, and your quality of work will be better, too.

3) Stand up and move around. If you can, get one of those standing work desks and use it at least half the time. If you alternate between standing and sitting you'll find that you're more alert and your brain works better.

4) Take a quick break every 20 minutes or so. 20 minute "bursts" of work followed by 2-3 minutes of non-work can make you productive and keep you and your brain energized. BEST: Do something physical on these short breaks like push-ups, sit-ups or deep knee bends.

5) Engage your senses. Use some peppermint or orange oil to wake you up. Make your work space interesting to look at with thought-provoking art. Use colored paper and pens. Get a worry stone or some kind of object you like to hold and

pick this up for tactile stimulation when you're thinking through a problem. I have a smooth rock I found on the beach that I like to flip over and over in my hand when I'm thinking or when I'm stressed, and it works like a charm.

6) Relax for 10 minutes every 90 – 120 minutes. Take 10 minutes off to meditate, walk around the block or work on a puzzle. Your brain will love this.

7) Work when your brain wants to work. Everyone has their own circadian rhythm. Some people are morning people, others are night owls, and many fall in between. Find out what time of day is your most productive and then schedule that time for your most intense and important work.

8) Prioritize. Work on your most important task first, when your brain is at its freshest. Getting this task done first will also give you a much needed feeling of accomplishment and free yourself up to focus on the lesser goals.

9) Work less, play more. Seriously, if you're working 100 hours a week then I suspect you're only doing 50 hours worth of work. Think about it – how much of your time is truly devoted to working, and how much is devoted to "getting ready to work?" Don't allow yourself to get distracted by emails, games, news, weather, etc. Instead focus yourself on getting your tasks done as quickly as possible, and then leave your computer, leave your office and go do something totally unrelated to work. While you are out "playing" your brain will be rejuvenating. One unexpected benefit to this is you'll

find your brain becomes more creative and a much better problem solver when it gets periods of rest, relaxation and diversion from work.

10) Take a weekly vacation. No, I'm not kidding. Getting away once a week does wonders for every part of you, especially your brain. And you don't have to leave your area to take a vacation. Go someplace locally you've never been to, take a class, go to events, spend the day walking downtown or in the woods, etc.

Is the weather terrible and you don't want to leave home? Then grab that book you've got of nature photographs or travel shots and sit in a comfortable chair and transport yourself to the exotic places you see in the photos. In terms of benefits to the brain, it's almost as good as being there.

11) Exercise. I'm not going to tell you all the reasons why you should exercise here – you probably already know them. And one of the biggest reasons is because when you exercise, your brain works better. You think better and more clearly. I wouldn't be a bit surprised if people who regularly exercise improve their IQ scores – it's already been proven to increase memory and comprehension.

12) Feed your brain. Good nutrition is vital to your brain's well-being. If you're eating processed foods or junk foods, you're starving your brain. If you're eating things like fresh fruits and vegetables and fish, then you're feeding your brain. Don't

believe me? Cut out all junk food and processed food for one week. Add in fish oils or fish, along with plenty of veggies and some fruits. See if you don't notice a massive difference in both the way you feel and how well your brain functions.

Be good to your brain and it will help you achieve and do more in life.

Wear a White Lab Coat to Make Less Typos

Under the heading of strange and bizarre, Adam and Galinsky tested the effect of wearing a white lab coat (like scientists wear) on people's powers of attention. Result? People wearing the white coats outperformed those who weren't. In fact, they made only half as many errors as those folks who were wearing their own clothes.

And while I can't lay my hands on the research right now, I also know that the act of putting on your workout clothes can put you in the right frame of mind for exercising. Even more interesting, I've known people who keep certain statues, coffee cups, a troll doll and even a yodeling pickle close by when they are working on their computers. Why? Apparently these items help them to think better.

So here's the idea: Figure out what clothes, hats, jewelry, items, etc. put you in the right frame of mind for working. Maybe you like to wear a writer's jacket and smoke a pipe? Maybe you like to place mirrors on your desk so you can talk ideas over with yourself? Or perhaps you'd like to try the white lab coat trick. Whatever your preference, if it enhances your work then by all means be a bit eccentric and just go for it.

Money Making Ideas Are EVERY Where – Just Ask Disappearing Romney

After Mitt Romney lost to Obama in the elections an enterprising person purchased http://DisappearingRomney.com/ and made a very simple page that shows how many people are "unfriending" Romney in real time.

How did he monetize it? At the bottom of the page he had Romney and Obama items that could be purchased from Amazon. Here's where it gets really interesting – the next day news agencies and bloggers all over the Internet were reporting on this website. In 24 hours Disappearing Romney received more free publicity than most websites get in a decade.

The lesson? Ideas are everywhere, you just have to look and or be creative. And when you get a great idea, jump on it FAST.

How to Out Run, Out Fox and Out Play Your Competition

You might only be interested in carving out a small niche online that earns you a nice five or six figure income, and that's fine. But if you want to run with the truly big (7+ figure) dogs, then there are some rules of business competition you need to know and practice to reach that level:

Rule #1: Respect your competition. Trash talking and disparaging your opponent brings down your own reputation and allows you to underestimate their real capability. Always assume that your competition is smarter and more resourceful than you are – that way you'll play at your highest level.

Rule #2: Use all of your resources and then some. If you only use your own ideas then you're limiting yourself and your business. Use the Internet, the media and the people you know to get new ideas. The more information you have, the better ideas you can come up with.

Rule #3: Check your ego at the door. It doesn't matter if your latest greatest idea came from you or your assistant or someone on television. What does matter is if it will put you ahead in the game or not. Just because it's your idea doesn't necessarily make it great, just as if it's someone else's idea doesn't necessarily make it bad.

Rule #4: Pursue the holy trinity of marketing. You want to find the convergence of need, entertainment and the new, surprising or unexpected. Making a memorable impact in your customer's mind in addition to providing a great product or service is what's going to put you ahead of your competition.

Rule #5: Play to win. Many businesses play to just survive, and that's not going to make you a competitor in the marketplace. Bring all of your resources and creativity to the table and play not to get through the day or to just keep up, but to win.

Stop Giving Away The Farm

People are a lot like sheep. Or lemmings. If they see the crowd going in a certain direction, they'll follow without even thinking about it. If that means diving off a cliff to their death, they'll do it. Metaphorically, of course. I'm hopeful that no one would really jump off a cliff just because the 50 people in front of them did it.

But if you're an independent thinker, it's good to ask if that crowd of sheep people is going in the right direction. For example, if everyone else is selling a stock, maybe you should buy it. Fortunes have been made with this one strategy alone. Sure, sometimes you'll lose your small investment, but that will be more than compensated for when it turns out you were right and everyone else was wrong. Just ask Warren Buffet.

Everyone else is competing on low price? Then charge the highest prices of all and offer the best service. Everyone else is tightening their belt and laying off people? What a great time to expand your business! Everyone else is shying away from buying a home? Now is when you will get the best selection at the best prices.

Which brings me to something we all do online to reel in new business – and that's to give stuff away. It used to be that we gave away little tastes of our products and services to entice people. Why not? It can be a good marketing strategy. Unless, of course, EVERYONE ELSE is doing it.

Then it becomes a competition to see who can give away more. Result? Consumers get a pile of stuff they don't look at, don't appreciate, don't care about, and it does them absolutely no good. We all know that the more we pay for something, the more we value it. You got it for free? Subconsciously (or even consciously) we assume it must be junk.

So the question becomes, are you going to continue to participate in this endless cycle of giving more and more away for free, hoping that it results in business down the road?

Or are you going to carefully tailor anything you give away to add to your bottom line?

Remember, no one wants to pay you for something you will give them for free. If you're selling a service and you give them a free consultation of custom tailored advice, why in the world would they then PAY you for what you've been giving them for free?

I know, it's a catch 22. You want to give them a taste so they'll come back for more, but you don't want to devalue you or your products and services in the eyes of the customer.

Which is why you want to focus more on telling people WHAT they need to do and not HOW to do it. Because when you show them what they need to do to accomplish their goals, they're now ready for the how-to steps of HOW to do it. Their appetite is whetted. And all you have to do is show them how to pay you.

I strongly suggest you pull back from giving away the farm. Let them see your success from the outside looking in, but if they want to see the inner workings, it's going to cost them. In the end they will be far better off for it, because having paid you for your information or services they will then be far more likely to appreciate it, use it and profit from it.

Shoes, Bras and Dolls - How to Keep Your Evergreen Content Fresh

I have heard of a place in the western U.S. which is miles from civilization and has a grove of trees deep in the forest that is filled with creepy dolls and worn out stuffed animals. You won't see this place advertised and it's extremely hard to find if you've never been there. Yet people make the trek into the wilderness just to see this grove of trees. Why are the trees filled with stuffed toys and cast away dolls? No one knows for sure.

Personally I've seen trees filled with shoes. Perhaps it starts with just one pair and grows from there. The benefit to shoes is if you tie them together by the shoestrings, you can fling a pair quite high into the air, thus eventually covering nearly the entire tree with old shoes. Stuffed toys and dollars don't weigh as much, so you've to place those by hand, filling the lower branches and leaving the higher reaches to those with climbing ability or ladders.

Then there's the bra tree south of Las Vegas, Nevada. Somehow it is seems appropriate to have a bra tree outside of Vegas because contrary to their slogan, you know that not everything that happens in Vegas really stays in Vegas. And again, people trek from all over to see this tree of bras that someone told them about.

Which brings us to our topic – evergreen content. People visit these trees in the heat of summer and blistery cold of winter, last year, this year and next year. And that's exactly what you want people to do with your evergreen content, as well. The problem, however, is that evergreen content tends to be dry. Just like a description of a tree, it's content that stands the test of time but won't be attracting much in the way of Tweets, Shares, Likes and so forth. No one gets excited about an ordinary grove of trees in Oregon because there are trees everywhere – but they do get excited if those trees are filled with eerie stuffed animals and dolls.

So here's how to make your evergreen content so good, people will go out of their way to visit it and tell others about it:

1. Give your posts personality. What makes the trees with dolls, bras and shoes stand out? They are different. They're unique. And above all they have personality. Inject your own personality into your writing to breathe life into it. You might not be able to fill it with shoes and bras, but you can find unique angles and ways of presenting your info that makes it highly interesting and worthy of sharing.
2. Write with your customer in mind. In fact, write as though you are speaking directly to your customer, who happens to also be a good friend of yours. Don't write like a textbook –

write like an email between friends.

3. Inject fun into your writing where ever it's appropriate. A little humor goes a long way to keeping your content fresh and memorable.

4. Illustrate with stories whenever possible. People love sharing stories with others almost as much as they love hearing or reading them.

5. Update your content. Dolls fall apart, bras and shoes fade. But because new dolls, bras and shoes are continually being placed in the trees, people keep coming. Your evergreen content works the same way. Go back every six months and update your content where ever it needs it so that it's still up to date and completely relevant to all the new changes that might have happened in the last few months. Not only will readers appreciate this, so will the search engines. Remember, Google loves fresh content, but that doesn't mean it has to be NEW content. Updating existing content can help you just as much in your rankings as writing entirely new posts and articles, and it's a lot easier to do.

6. Keep track of your content. You might create an inventory of all of your articles and blog posts. This will help you to stay organized, it will reveal the gaps in your content that you need to fill, and it will show you which content likely needs updating.

7. Do use dates. A common trick in blogging is to not display the date your content was posted. This way an article that's

several years old might be mistaken as being new – which frankly could be a bad thing for you. First, if you're not using dates then some visitors will wonder how old all of your content is and whether any of it is up to date. Second, someone reading a 4 year old article on SEO that hasn't been updated might think you don't know what you're talking about, since there have been so many changes since then. Instead of omitting dates, use the date of your last update. If you wrote an article a year ago but you've just gone through it and brought it completely up to date, there's no reason not to put today's date on it. All of the backlinks to that article will remain in place, and your readers will know that your content is current.

8. Do the unexpected. No one expects bras in trees – hence people flock to see it. Surprise your audience and they will tell others to view your content, regardless of when it was written.

Re-Brand Yourself Into Having No Competition

You've chosen a great niche with lots of demand and lots of competition, which means there's lots of money to be made. Next step? Re-brand yourself so that you no longer have any real competition. Call yourself and your business something that no one else owns.

For example, there are tons of marketing consultants and branding experts and social media experts and so forth, so you don't want to call yourself by the same title as a million other people.

Instead, become a marketing funnel expert, or a conversion consultant. Or even create your own marketing niche, such as Guerrilla Marketing, Duct Tape Marketing and Purple Cows. Think of it this way - You want to be #1 at something new, versus #100 at something old.

How to Get Viral Traffic With Very Little Effort

Here's an awesome traffic trick from Mike Stezlner of Social Media Examiner:

Write a blog post asking your readers to nominate their favorite ___. You fill in the blank. It might be their favorite blog, favorite Kindle book, favorite video – whatever you choose. Tell them you're doing the Top 10 so you can have 10 winners instead of 1.

Here's the trick – require that every nominee must have at least TWO nominations to be considered (or 3 if you're ambitious.) This ensures that your contest goes viral. For example, if I want to nominate a blog and make sure it gets considered, I'll email or tweet someone else and ask them to hit up your site and nominate the same blog.

To take this to the next level, get 3 well-known judges from your niche. These should be names most people in your niche easily recognize. How do you get them? Email them all simultaneously, asking them, "Would you be willing to be a judge on a panel with expert #2 and expert #3?" You're using social proof to get them to agree, and you are being completely honest at the same time.

Write a second post announcing the finalists as determined by the judges. You can even do a second round by having the judges pick 25 finalists and getting your readers to do the voting.

Get custom badges designed for the top 10 that they can put on their websites. Everyone loves recognition. And be sure to place a link back to YOUR website in the badges. (Clever, huh?)

You'll get 10 happy winners plus tons of traffic and awareness.

Don't Sell – Do This Instead

Say that you have got a great ebook on dating for women, so you talk about how they'll get dates with amazing guys, right? That will work. But what will work even better is if you tell them their story – the story of how ever since they were little girls they've been waiting for the love of their life, their prince charming, and how your product will finally make that little girl's dream come true.

You've got a great ebook on making money, so you talk about the easy money, the fast cars, the mansion they'll buy. Sure, that will make some sales for you. But do you know what will work even better? Telling them the story of how they've struggled, how they've always felt a little bit like a failure because they couldn't afford the 2 weeks at baseball camp their son wanted, or the music lessons their daughter wants. Tell them the story of how their in-laws always looked down on them because they're weren't a good provider. Tell them the story of fearing they couldn't make the next house payment, or of being afraid to pick up the phone for fear it's a debt collector, or of lying awake at night wondering if their daughter's friends would all go off to college while their daughter worked as a waitress all her life.

Offering benefits sells. Telling stories sells even better.

404 Error Page Profits

No matter how hard you try to prevent it, sooner or later you'll have prospects land on your 404 error page. When they do, they have a choice – try to find what they were looking for or give up. Care to guess what happens more often? That's right, they leave in frustration. So instead of the usual "Whoops! We're sorry but what you're looking for has moved" page, consider customizing your error pages to get them to do something.

For example, you could give them an option to opt into your list with an offer that is different than your landing page. This can be highly effective. "Congrats! You just found our secret page where we give away ___. Just tell us where to send it and it's yours." Or you might make them an offer they can't refuse, such as a great deal on one of your most popular products, or a combination offer for a super low price. "Oops! You just landed on our error page, but we're going to make it up to you. Here's $xx.xx off of our super hot selling __."

Are You Guilty of Perpetrating Random Acts of Marketing?
There is an expression that accurately illustrates the strategy of far too many marketers: "Throw it against the wall and see if it sticks." They are continually trying this and that, hopping from one social media venue to another, one method to another, with no real strategy or idea of what they are doing. The result is they enjoy only sporadic success if not failure.

If this sounds like you, I challenge you to create a marketing strategy for yourself right now. Sit down with pen and paper and write – on one page – your strategy for marketing your product or service. You might not know what the best strategy is, but that's not even important at this point. Just get something down and then begin following it consistently and persistently. Make consistent, significant weekly progress based on your marketing plan.

For example, what method(s) are you going to use to get new prospects? How, where and when are you going to use these methods? What is the first action you want a prospect to take, or what is the first thing you do for that prospect? How do you follow up? And so forth.

When you see something is working, adjust your strategy to do more of that. If something isn't working, remove it from your strategy. But ALWAYS keep a one page record of your current working strategy and stick to it. When you make a change, make a new page and keep it at your desk or work area.

In my experience having this one page marketing strategy will do a great deal to focus your efforts and reduce your frustration of endlessly spinning your wheels and getting no where. A marketing strategy creates structure. Structure creates freedom since you know what you will do therefore you will not be distracted, or jump from one thing to another due to frustration. Lack of structure creates chaos.

2. Time Management Hacks

Goof Off and Get More Done

One thing I've noticed is that if I take a five minute break every hour or so, I tend to feel more refreshed and also get more work done. The trick of course is to not let the 5 minutes extend into a half hour or more, so here are a few ideas that are quick and helpful...

1. Jump. Get a rebounder (mini trampoline) and put it in your office. Every hour or so go jump on it. Your head will clear, your muscles will get worked and you'll feel energized.
2. Play. Whether it's a remote control helicopter you fly around your office or an old Rubik's Cube, find something you can do for 5 minutes and then put it down. Not recommended: Video games. We all know that 5 minutes on a video game can easily turn into 2 hours, so save those for when your work is done.

3. Yoga or any stretching type of exercise to feel invigorated and less stressed.

4. Mind games. Here's a site I like... http://GamesForTheBrain.com Check out the game, "Guess the colors."

5. Online jigsaw puzzles. Sign up at http://Jigzone.com and they'll send you a new puzzle everyday.

6. Walking. Take two or three laps around your house or up and down a staircase.

7. Cleaning or straightening. Find something small that needs attention and takes no more than 5 minutes. You'll feel productive and glad to get back to work.

How To Get More Done In Less Time

You're only as successful as your performance today. Because the better your productivity, the more you get done. And the more you get done, the faster your business grows. Not to mention the fact that if you can get all of your work done in 6 hours instead of 12, you now have 6 more hours in which you can either play or grow your business even larger.

No matter what you're doing, if you're productive you're not only building your business - you're also gaining confidence. And studies show you're also happier. After all, what feels better – relaxing at the end of a day in which you accomplished nothing, or a day in which you did everything you set out to do?

One more thing about being productive - the faster you get a task done, the more likely you are to want to do that task again. For example, if it takes you 3 hours to write one article, the next time you want to write an article you're going to be sorely tempted to procrastinate because you remember what a long, tedious, arduous process it was for you last time. But if you can crank out an excellent article in 15 minutes, then the next time you write an article you'll be enthusiastic and ready to jump in with both feet.

No matter how you look at it, being productive is a tremendous help to you, your business and your mindset. So what are some simple ways to get more done in less time?

Set a timer. Whatever it is that you need to do, set a time limit in which you will accomplish the task and allow nothing to distract you. Keep an eye on the timer so you can gauge your progress, and when the time goes off you are finished.

This single tip alone can double or even triple your productivity because work invariably expands to fill the time we allot to it. If we allot 5 hours, it will take 5 hours. But if we only allot 90 minutes, then that's how long it will almost certainly take.

And surprisingly, the work performed in the shorter time frame tends to be equal or even surpass the quality of work performed in the longer time frame. Perhaps this is because we do not allow distractions to derail our performance when we know we're under a time crunch.

Set a measurable goal each and every day, and then STICK to it.
Don't worry about long terms goals - the marketplace changes so
rapidly that any long term goal is likely irrelevant. Instead, focus on
short term goals – specifically, what exactly are you going to
accomplish today?

Write it down, keep it in front of you, and at the end of the day ask
yourself one question: "Did I meet my goal or not?" There are only 2
possible answers and absolutely no room for excuses because you
either did or you did not. If you met your goal, congratulations – you
did exactly what you set out to do. Now set another goal for
tomorrow. If you did not accomplish your goal, determine what went
wrong and do not make the same mistake twice.

Accountability partners. Having a daily goal forces you to become
more productive, and if you want to put this technique on steroids,
get yourself an accountability partner. This is someone you phone or
email your daily goal(s) to, and then at the end of the day you report
back and tell them if you succeeded or failed in meeting those goals.
Better yet, start an accountability group. There's something about
having an entire group of people keeping you accountable that will
cause you to move heaven and earth to not only meet, but exceed
your daily goals.

Forget perfection. If you're one of those folks who can't send an
email or launch a product until it's perfect, then it's high time you got
over yourself. Trying to be perfect is just another form of

procrastination – an excuse to not get your work done until it's just right, which it never is. This is the Internet, and doing things well enough is far, far better than not doing it at all.

People who email you want an answer now, not a perfect answer 3 days from now. People looking for solutions to their problems want to buy your product now, not in 6 months when you've proof read it a dozen times. And if you simply can't seem to get past the need to make things perfect, then try this – procrastinate about being perfect. Tell yourself you will go back later and make it perfect, but for right now you're launching this product or making this blog post or whatever. And if you're worried about the nitpickers out there who will email you about the typo on page 22, place this disclaimer in all of your products and on your websites:

"Did you find a typo on this page? Congratulations! Sometimes I'm in such a hurry to get this great information to you that I make little mistakes along the way. Go ahead and email me the typo if you like, and thanks so much for paying attention – you're the best!"

Those who feel it is their duty to find typos will feel applauded and may spend even more time on your web page reading your info and searching for more typos (they'll love this!) And you know what? It's like getting your proofreading done for free. Sly, I know. As for the vast majority who just don't care about typos – they may have a good chuckle when they read this disclaimer and remember the last time someone pointed out their typos to them.

Impose the immovable deadline on yourself. Let's say you want to create a new product: Determine how long it will take you and then email your list and let them know exactly when it will be ready. Better yet, get a fellow marketer to announce a webinar complete with sign-ups. For example, you're creating a new product and you figure it will take you 48 hours. Either email your list or get another marketer to email their list announcing that you're doing a webinar on the topic in 3 days or less.

Now you MUST finish the product on time or you won't have anything to prsent and offer on the webinar. Begin creating your product by starting with the very best information first, and working your way down the information hierarchy from most important to least important. This way if you don't get it all in, it won't matter anyway because you will have the most important info in place, and that's what your customers want anyway.

Do you realize you could create 2 new products per WEEK using this method? Now what would that do for your bottom line?

Just-in-Time Learning
Quick tip: Don't buy an Info product unless you know you're going to use at least one piece of information inside that product immediately. For example, you're creating a forum and you see a product on how to get people really active inside your forum and you know you'll use that product immediately, so you buy it. You're making your money back on that product almost immediately.

But then you see a great looking product on how to do webinars, but you don't do webinars and you have no immediate plans to do any in the future. Should you buy it? After all, you may use it down the road and you may make money from it, right? I think you already know the answer from your past experiences – don't buy it. All you have to do is look at your hard drive at all the products you've purchased in the past that you haven't touched to know that unless you're going to use the product immediately, odds are very good you will never use it.

Because what happens? A year from now you decide to do webinars. Great. The only thing is, you've totally forgotten that webinar product you bought a year ago. Or you remember it, spend a half hour searching for it, only to discover halfway the info in it is outdated and you would have been better offer buying a new info product on webinars.

You can see why I call this just-in-time learning. You buy an info product just in time to learn from it and USE THAT INFO to further your business. You'll be surprised how much money you'll save this way, and how much more you'll earn from the products you actually do purchase.

Movement is Better Than Meditation
Joe Polish tells a great Gary Halbert story about the power of taking action, even when you're not sure of what you're doing. And if you

sell big ticket items or ever plan to, this story also has a great strategy for quadrupling your sales as well.

Gary visited Joe at his office in Arizona one day and gave Joe some advice on a profitable mailing campaign Joe was running. Gary told Joe that if he would simply follow up with phone calls to each prospect, he would quadruple the amount of sales he was making. And since it was a very high-priced item they were selling, it would be insane for Joe NOT to do it.

Joe agreed it was a good idea, but did Joe do it? No.So a month later when Gary comes to visit again, he instructs Joe to withdraw $21,000 in $50 bills from the bank, which Joe does. Obviously Joe trusted Gary a great deal for him to simply withdraw all of this money in cash and hand it over to Gary.

So what does Gary do? He calls a team meeting of Joe's people. With everyone gathered around the table, Gary starts ripping the bands off each stack of bills and throwing them up in the air and screaming, "You might as well piss away this $1,000, you might as well piss away this $1,000, and just keeps throwing money up and screaming. "Every day you sit here and you don't make phone calls, you might as well throw away $1,000, so get off your ass and make these calls and that means every single one of you, and don't be bitching about how you need to make more money when you're sitting working on all kinds of other crap that isn't making you any money. All you have to do is just simply pick up the damn phone and call the people that you sent the letter to and say, "Hey, I sent you a letter, would you like to buy ___?" If you do that, and that alone, you're going to increase your sales." *Gary was always rather direct in his communication. :-)*

So Joe rented a hotel room and stuck three temporary employees in there making phones calls. Result? They made a bunch of sales and a ton of cash. See? You don't have to know everything before you do something. It's better to jump on that phone and say something stupid to a prospect than to never speak to that prospect at all.

I once read the autobiography of an insurance salesman who was perhaps the shyest, quietest person in the world. But what he could do was pick up a phone, call somebody and say, "I don't suppose you want to buy any insurance, do you?" The guy made millions. I've also heard similar stories about new car salesmen who copied this same technique: "You don't want to buy a car, do you?"

Of course they could have waited until they had more confidence, until they got their sales speech down perfect, until they had an answer for every objection. But instead, they simply got to work without over thinking anything.

Movement is better than meditation. So get moving – you'll be surprised by the doors that begin opening for you when you do.

3. List Building And Email Marketing Hacks

Why I Can't Send You The Report

If you're using double-opt-in in your list building, you know that a certain percentage who sign onto your list will never confirm their email address. These are subscribers that you've earned and yet you lose them anyway. So how can you increase the number of people who click that confirmation link to join your list? David Dutton has a great idea. Instead of using the subject line, "Confirm your email address," he uses, "Why I can't send you the 'marketing results guaranteed' daily tips."

This takes the freebie away from the new potential subscriber. Now instead of thinking... "Hmm, did I *really* want that report?" They're thinking, "HEY! GIMME MY REPORT RIGHT NOW!!!" Almost nothing motivates like fear of loss. I know in my case my hand raced to open that email and click the confirmation link – despite the fact that *I knew* I was being psychologically played like a ten dollar fiddle. So just imagine how well it can work in niches outside of online marketing.

Want Your Emails To Get Opened? Then Do THIS

What's the difference between a television series and a television movie? The movie is over in 2 hours, of course, while the series carries on week after week. Now what's the difference between an ordinary TV series and a soap opera? On a regular TV series, there is resolution by the end of each show. The viewer is satisfied that this particular story is complete. So why do they tune in the following week? Because they like the characters and the stories. This keeps them coming back for more.

But with a soap opera there is no completion at the end of each episode. Instead, the viewer is always left with one or more cliffhangers which sticks in their minds. They are left wondering what happens next? So the next day those same viewers are eagerly watching their soap opera again, because they're dying to know what happened. Problem is, every show is a cliffhanger, and so they get addicted to the show.

Now imagine that soap opera is your email series – every day readers open their email to get resolution to something you wrote yesterday, such as the end to a story. But then you start a new story and you don't tell them the end until tomorrow. You get the point. It doesn't have to be stories, it can be anything that makes the reader desperately want to know the piece of information you're withholding until the next email.

For example, "Tomorrow I'll tell you the 3 secret words to doubling conversion on every one of your salesletters." Or, "Tomorrow I'll reveal the 5 common household products that, when combined and added to your soil, grow the biggest, sweetest tomatoes you've ever tasted."

Do this every time and you'll see your email open rate skyrocket. Want to see this concept illustrated in video form? Check out this mesmerizing video of little-people dressed as clowns and desperately chasing this guy across the globe.

Find Writing Inspiration in the Oddest of Places

Recently I saw an old Cosmopolitan Magazine from over 10 years ago. Curious, I looked inside and there I found a large 36 page pullout booklet on astrology. Now before you roll your eyes, stay with me a moment. Intrigued by my discovery, I started paging through and realized I was holding what could potentially be a copywriting swipe file gold mine.

For example, inside the front cover were predictions for the coming year for each of the 12 signs. For example:

"The months ahead are packed with amazing change-your-life opportunities. Find out when you'll: Access extra cash, go on a wild road trip, blaze trails in the bedroom and boardroom."

"Clear your head for the choices that await you. Look inside to find out how you to decide between: A dream job and a promotion, two potential bedmates, sparing a friend's feelings while telling her the truth."

"This year, you'll hit so many highs, you'll need an oxygen mask. Here's a preview of what awaits you: Primo professional perks, an off-the-charts and surprising sexual affair, an incredible image upgrade."

47

And that was just the first 3 of 12 predictions, and just the first page of writing.

Look at the first sentence in each paragraph again. Don't these read like the lead in's to sales letters or hot blog posts? Let's try swiping some of the copy to promote a resumé service, making only minor changes:

"Keep Reading To Discover How Small Tweaks To Your Resume Can Give You An Incredible Image Upgrade, Your Dream Job And A Big Promotion With Primo Professional Perks."

Or a make money product:

"Online Marketers: The Months Ahead Will Be Packed With Amazing Change-Your-Life Opportunities – If You Take The Right Steps Now."

Or a dating product for guys:

"This Year, Your Dating Will Hit So Many Highs, You'll Need An Oxygen Mask. Here's A Preview Of What Awaits You: Off-The-Charts And Surprising Sexual Affairs, Your Unending Pick Of Bed Mates, And New Trails Blazed In The Bedroom And Boardroom."

If you're not already accumulating a swipe file, I suggest you start immediately. Anytime and anywhere you find good material, put it in your file to reference the next time you need to write some copy. And don't look at just sales letters and blog posts – look at everything, including material outside of your niche.

3 Systems to Build Your List AND Make Money

I'm often asked two questions: "How do I build my list?" and "How do I make money quickly?" To most these seem like two entirely different problems, yet there are at least three solutions that can do both for you simultaneously...

Method #1: Give a Product Away Virally Attract Affiliates Build Your List of Buyers AND Make Money

You're going to give a product away, and then you're going to ask the people you give the product to if they would like to SELL it for 100% instant commissions.

First, give the product out in exchange for testimonials and add those testimonials to the sales page. Now set the product at a low price, $5 to $10, and ask everyone you gave the product to if they would like to promote it for instant 100% commissions. Be sure to either place your affiliate link inside your product that sells another product, or place a link to another one of your products.

Keep in mind that anyone can promote your product - even if they don't have a list or a website – simply by sending out tweets or talking about it on Facebook. On the download page, you're going to offer buyers the opportunity to promote the product and earn 100% instant commissions. This will keep a steady stream of new affiliate coming in and promoting your product.

You're virally building your email list full of BUYERS, and you're making money from that link you placed inside your product.

BONUS: Also place your money making link on the download page, but be sure that the offer to promote your product for 100% commission takes precedence on the page. It's more important to build your list of buyers than to make quick cash, because that list of buyers will pay you over and over again.

SMART MOVE: Use your affiliate link inside the product and on the download page to promote a continuity program such as a membership or ongoing software program. This way you make extra money for several months or more, all from this one effort.

Method #2: Sell a Written Product for Cheap Give Buyers Access To Live Course Ask Them To Promote For You

This time you're selling your report or other info product for $5 to $7 just to get as many sales as possible. Collect your testimonials and add it to the sales page, and now upgrade the product to a live training for 7 to 20 times the price.

Let all of your report buyers know that they will get the training for FREE, and ask them to promote the training for you at 50-75% commission. All they have to do is send people to your free webinar.

You hold the webinar, give out some great info and then promote the offer. Nothing closes more sales than live webinars because the listeners get a real feel for you and what you're offering. Again you're building your list of buyers and making money.

Method #3 Contact Forum Owner Offer 100% Commissions Recruit Buyers Into Affiliates

This is similar to Method #1, except this time instead of giving your product away, you're going to contact forum owners (and website owners, too) and offer them 100% instant commissions if they will promote your product in banner ads on their website.

On the one time offer page, instead of making an OTO, you'll offer the buyers a chance to sell the product for 100% commissions. Then make the same offer on the download page. Add in an affiliate link on the download page and inside the product so you make some quick cash, too.

In methods #1 and #3, the top priority is building a list of buyers you can promote to over and over again, and the second priority is making some money.

Method #2 reverses this. If you're selling a $97 training at 50% commission, you can make some serious money fairly quickly. And you'll still be building your list – in fact you'll have three lists: The first list is everyone who purchased your inexpensive info product. The second list is all those who signed up for your initial webinar, and the third is a sub list of those who purchased the actual training product.

As you can see, it's not rocket science to simultaneously build your list and make money. And even a new marketer can do this. One caveat: You need software that allows for instant payout of commissions.

8 Email Marketing Mistakes That Cost You Sales and Subscribers

1) **Being boring.** I'm placing this at number one because it's the biggest mistake of all and I want you to remember it. After you write your email, reread it. If it bores you, just imagine what it will do to your readers. Be compelling, be interesting, be funny, be passionate, be crazy – in short, be ANYTHING but boring.

2) **Burying your message.** In journalism they call it burying the lead – that is, hiding the most important information deep inside your email instead of placing it at the top.

3) **Lousy personalization.** You've received emails that said, "Dear ____" or "Dear #firstname#. Gee, wasn't that swell? Don't do it to your readers. No personalization is far better than mistakes like these.

4) **Sending only solicitation emails.** Sure you want your list to buy stuff, but if you only send "BUY THIS" type of emails, your list will think you only love them for their money and they'll stop opening your emails. Mix in interesting informational emails with your ads, and surprise your readers whenever you can.

5) **Telling them what they already know**. If your message begins with information just about everyone on your list already knows, you'll bore them into deleting your message

before you ever get to the point.

6) **Lack of focus.** If the purpose of your email is to sell a product, then don't make more than one offer in that email or you'll confuse them into inaction.

7) **Stuck in a rut timing.** So you always send out messages on Tuesday and Thursday mornings because somebody somewhere told you that's the best time? How do they know? Test different days and different times to see what works for you.

8) **Lack of call to action.** Don't tell them to "Click here to learn more." Be specific on what they can expect to find on the other side of that click and why it's imperative that they go there now (in other words, what's in it for them?)

9) **Being boring.** Yes, I said this before, but it bears repeating. DO NOT BORE YOUR LIST OR THEY WILL STOP READING YOUR EMAILS. Nuff said.

10 Email Subject Lines

Next time you're stuck for a subject line, just refer to this handy reference guide:

The Big Benefit: You already know to emphasize benefits over features, but are you placing your biggest benefit in your subject lines? Try it and if the benefit matches a major desire of your list, you'll likely see your open rate go through the roof.

How-to: This one is easy and effective – use your subject line to indicate you're going to reveal how to do something they are likely to want to do. "How to lose 5 pounds today," "How to make $100 this afternoon," etc.

The Urgency Factor: Create some anxiety and get your email opened. You can do this two different ways – first by showing them what they gain by taking immediate action, such as gaining a free Kindle book today only. Second by demonstrating what they lose if they don't act, such as losing entry into a program that is closing shortly.

The Numbered List: There is something almost magical about using numbers in subject lines and headlines, plus it gives you a road map to write the content that follows. For example: "Top 10 reasons why you're doing email marketing all wrong" or "5 ways to get your children to behave."

Keyword Bait: If you've built a targeted list, then there are certain keywords that will likely get your emails opened by that list. For example, if your list is made up of horse lovers, then you're going to want words like horse, colt, foal, mare, riding etc. in most of your emails since they act as triggers for your readers.

Discover Astounding Secrets: Benefits plus curiosity are always a winner. Use words such as discover, secrets, amazing, astonishing, etc.

Ask a question: A question irresistibly compels the reader to think and answer. "Is he the right man for you?" "Would personal coaching help you achieve your goals?"

The Eyebrow Raiser: If you can get them intrigued enough to raise an eyebrow, they will open your email. For example: "Why chickens are master gardeners," "The couch potato's guide to weight loss" and "5 foods that make you LOSE weight."

The Story Starter: Everybody loves a good story, so if your subject line sounds like it's leading into a story, people will click it. "This morning my son asked me where babies come from" and "My client was hopping mad."

The Curiosity Raiser: You're not telling them much of anything in the subject line, yet you still make them curious enough to open it. How? By raising their curiosity. "This is B.S.," "Never again," "What was I thinking?," etc.

4. Product Creation Hacks

Super Fast Product Creation With Immediate Sales

How can you create a product in less than a week that has a high perceived value and is almost guaranteed to bring its own traffic and sales? One word: Interviews. Here's how to do it...

First, choose a niche if you don't already have one. Preferably you want to find a niche with experts *who have their own email lists.* Second, choose a hook. If your niche is vegetable gardening, your hook might be, "How to grow an entire years worth of veggies for less than $50." If your niche is classic cars, your hook might be, "How to buy classic cars for half their real value." If your niche is Internet Marketing, your hook might be, "How to drive tons of traffic to your website without spending a dime."

Third, once you have your hook you'll want to find your experts. Book authors are great for this, as are bloggers and any fairly well-known experts in your niche. Don't be afraid to approach well known people because you're going to offer them something they want – exposure. Everyone has something they want to plug, whether it's their latest book, their website, their new product or whatever - and you're going to use this to your advantage.

Fourth, contact your experts. You can do this through phone or email, whichever you're more comfortable with. Ask them if you can interview them, and be sure to mention that you want to plug their latest product or book for several minutes at the end of the interview. Everyone loves a chance to not only expand their audience, but to also make some sales of their latest product.

Fifth, if their product has an affiliate program you'll want to sign up as an affiliate, do a redirect and give that link at the end of the interview to promote the product. This way both you and your interview subject will make money.

Sixth, conduct the interview. Sign up for a trial at Instant Teleseminar (http://instantteleseminar.com/). You'll get your own conference number and access code. Set the interview up to be recorded, and once the interview is over you can download the mp3 recording. Simple!

Keep the interview fun and relaxed, and ask questions along the lines of your hook. You might want to let your interview subject know ahead of time what you will be asking so they can be properly prepared. They might also have suggestions for you on what they would like you to ask them.

Seventh, ask your interview subjects to promote your new interview product for you. Because they are one of the featured speakers they will most likely not only promote it, but promote it heavily. In addition to sales for you and commissions for them; it also means subscriber sign ups for you and back end sales as well (remember, you're promoting a product at the end of each interview and receiving affiliate commissions on those as well.)

And there you have it – an easy, fast way to create your own product with a high perceived value. If you do a dozen or so interviews, you can easily charge $47 to $97 for the package. And since you've chosen experts who have their own mailing lists, you'll also have a way to promote your product for immediate sales while simultaneously growing your list!

4 Ways To Create Products Super Fast

Almost nothing is better than having your own product because you not only keep 100% of the sale price with you sell it – you can also get affiliates to sell it for you, thus simultaneously building your list and bank account through the efforts of others.

And then there's the Warrior Forum – get Warrior Special Offer (WSO) of the Day and you could see your list of buyers swell by a couple of thousand or more. A Warrior Special Offer of the Day is a product that has generated a large volume of sells in the Warrior Special Offer forum. WSO forum is a where various info products are sold at a special (discount) price.

So how do you crank out products quickly and easily that people are hungry to buy? I've compiled a list of proven methods – and none of these should take you longer than 7 days, with most taking only a few hours.

Interview an Expert. This is a super fast and easy way to create a product, and you don't need to have any expertise of your own. Instead you're "borrowing" the subject's knowledge and packaging it into a product.

So where do you find these experts?

1. Search Amazon for authors in your niche – authors are often eager for the chance to share their knowledge and plug their latest book, and so they're open to being interviewed. And on Amazon you can find an author on just about any niche topic you want to pursue.

2. If you're in the IM niche, search the Warrior Forum for knowledgeable marketers. Warrior Special Offer Pro (WSO Pro) will show you who has WSO's that are selling well. Also consider interviewing the Warriors who get WSO of the Day. To get WSO of the Day they have to pass stringent criteria, thus they tend to stand apart from the crowd of product creators on the Forum.

3. Look for authors on Clickbank. Clickbank is broken into niches so it's easy to search. Choose your niche and look at the gravity of each product within that niche to find something with a high gravity (100+). This means that the product is selling well, and this might be a good person to interview.

4. Do case studies. This is a bit different because instead of interviewing your subject on his expertise, you're asking

specifically how s/he did one particular thing. For example, interviewing someone with a best selling WSO or who received WSO of the day on how they put their product together and how they achieved their success.

Use What You Know by Recording Your Own Tips and Tricks. You may not think you have skills that others want to learn, but odds are you do. Maybe you know how to write a great blog post in 10 minutes, or how to lose 50 pounds in 3 months, or how to swap out the engine on a '57 Chevy.

You can either turn this knowledge into a report or ebook, or record it as videos or audios. Once you start breaking down what you do step-by-step, you might be surprised at how much you know. And if there's a market for what you know, you've got yourself a viable product.

Don't ever discount your own knowledge. If you're in the IM niche, for example, and you've only been working in it for six months, you still know things that people who are just starting out don't know, and those things can be turned into your own unique product. You don't have to be the foremost expert in a niche – you can simply have more knowledge than the customers you'll be targeting.

Turn Your Existing Content into New Products. Have you written a bunch of articles and blog posts? Maybe you've got enough there to create your own book. Do you have videos that you've made, audios, etc? Can you package this content into a product?

Repurposing your own content is a great way to make a completely self-created product very quickly.

Co-Create a Product with Someone Else. Team up with someone who has the skills you don't and vice versa. Perhaps you're a good writer and they have the knowledge, or you have the personality to make the videos and they have the background in the niche. Decide in the beginning what needs to be done and who will do what, and the deadline for completion.

The benefits here are two-fold: First, two heads and two sets of experience are better than one. And second, by working as a team you are accountable to each other, and the product is likely to get created quite quickly with no procrastination or stalling getting in the way.

How to Create a Product That Sells

Notice the headline doesn't say, "How to Create a Product and Sell It." Frankly, that's exactly what most marketers do – they create a product without any thought to what the market wants, and then they try to figure out a way to sell it. Result? 4 times out of 5, failure.

To create a product that sells, you want to first identify a niche that's hungry, and then offer them whatever it is that they are hungry for. The hard work is in finding that target audience that is ready and eager to buy.

Once you've done that, creating the product is the easy part, as well as the fun part because you know in advance that you are about to make money.

So how do you identify a hungry niche?

Here are keys to look for when investigating a possible market:

- Are they in pain? Are they seeking relief from that pain, and are they willing to pay for that relief?
- Do they have a problem? If so, are they willing to pay to get the solution to that problem?
- Are they seeking a specific pleasure? Are they willing to pay to receive that pleasure?

My advice is to focus as much as possible on the first two. While people are certainly willing to pay for pleasure, they will part with their money far faster to relieve pain or solve a pressing problem.

If you find competition in your prospective niche, it's a good sign that there is money to be made, so don't think you've got to find some great undiscovered niche – it's not likely to happen. If there is no competition, realize that it's probably because no one is buying.

Now then, you are going to allow your market niche to define your product. In other words, rather than creating the product and finding the market, you've now found your market and you're going to create your product to satisfy the specific needs of that market.

Let's say you're targeting retirees who want to make extra income online. What do you know about your niche? You know that generally they're not as computer savvy as teens and twenty-somethings, that they're going to be more receptive to building long term income rather than something that's supposed to make them rich overnight, that they're likely to be more skeptical when it comes to making money from home, and so forth.

Thus you are going to target all of your marketing and your products using the information you gather from your research on this niche, and you're going to always have your prospects in mind when you're working on your business. You might even imagine a couple of your best prospects right there in the room with you as you're creating your product and your marketing materials.

Let me give you a head start on finding a niche that's just dying to purchase your product.

The three biggest, hottest and hungriest mega niches are...

1. Health, fitness and weight loss
2. Making money
3. Relationships, dating and personal development

These are excellent starting points, but of course you're not going to target the ENTIRE health, fitness and weight loss market. If you're trying to market to everyone, you are marketing to NO ONE. Thus you're going to drill down to find the specific group within these niches that you want to market to.

Examples: College women wanting to lose weight. Stay at home Mom's wanting to earn money. People married over 10 years wanting to put the spark back in their marriage. And you could narrow it down from there. The point is, once you have a hungry niche, you extensively research and even interview that niche until you know exactly what they want, and then offer it to them.

Do you see the difference between guessing what people might want, and KNOWING in advance what they will pay for? It will save you time and frustration while growing your bank account 10 times faster than guessing ever would. Next, I'm going to share my product creation outline with you. This is the outline I like to use when I'm creating any kind of an info product, as it makes the writing go fast and I don't forget anything important.

Hint: If you need to create a product in the next 48 hours? Use this outline!

Product Creation Outline

You want to create a product but the process seems daunting. Been there. Felt that. But you know what? There are shortcuts. Rather than struggling to figure out what to write (or say, if you're making a video) why not follow a proven outline?

No matter what your topic, no matter what your niche, I think you'll find this universal outline is a tremendous help for creating great products quickly, with the least fuss, hassle and sweat. And NO tears. With this formula, even sworn non-writers can create their own products.

Let's get started.

1. Set the Scene.

You're going to tell them who you are, how it is that you know what you're talking about (or writing about) and the results they can expect to get from your product. In other words, you're providing your credentials that allow you to teach them about this topic and you're telling them what they're going to learn.

Example: My name is John Dee and I've been an online marketer for 10 years now. In that time I went from struggling newbie to making a full time income from my online endeavors, and I want to teach you how to do the very same. Imagine if, by following the system you're about to discover, you can quit your job just 6 months from now and live the life you've always dreamed of. If you're willing to put in the time and effort, you can make your dream a reality.

2. Warn them of Challenges

Tell them what their challenges and obstacles will be to getting the results they're seeking. Let them know you understand what they're going through, their problem, etc. You're creating a bond here between you and your reader or listener. You're also letting them know that they have to put in the effort to get the results. Just because they purchased your product doesn't mean they're done –

they're only getting started. Let them know there's work to do and you'll show them exactly what that work is.

3. Tell Your Story

Hopefully you have your own story of how you had this same challenge or problem and how you over came it. People love stories and they especially want to know that a) you had the same challenge and b) using what they're about to learn, you overcame that challenge.

4. Tell Them What NOT To Do.

Are there myths or out of date thinking that they might need to be aware of? Perhaps methods that don't work, old wives tales, etc.? Let them know what doesn't work and why it doesn't work. You're telling them what's been holding them back from success and you're giving them the chance to release their old beliefs and ideas so they can readily embrace what you're about to teach them.

5. Give Them The Goods

This is the main body of your work, where you will be teaching them all about your topic. This is the biggest section and you'll find it's far easier to create if you first make an outline of what you're teaching and then fill in that outline.

6. Pitfalls

Whatever you're teaching, there are going to be pitfalls and mistakes they need to avoid. What are they, and how do they avoid or overcome them? What are the hurdles? How can they bypass the challenges or at least be ready to deal with them?

7. The Starting Point

By now your reader may be feeling overwhelmed so give them a starting point. This is where you gently push them towards the door and tell them what their first destination/goal/activity is on the road to reaching the outcome they seek. And you're done! You can use this product outline to create reports, ebooks, videos, audios – even a book you sell on Amazon. By using this outline your work goes a great deal faster and you won't stare at your blank computer screen, wondering what to write.

10 Places To Find A Great Idea For Your Next Info Product

Are you stuck for ideas? Maybe you're not sure what niche you want to go into next, or you've got the niche but you don't know what your next product should be. Here are 10 ideas to get you started...

1. Use Your Job Experience. Do you have a particular skill, expertise or career experience that people would pay to learn more about? Maybe you've managed and led corporate teams to accomplish extraordinary things. Or maybe you were the best chef in the city. Whatever your job experience, there might be people out there who would gladly pay to benefit from it.

2. Teach Something. If there is a topic you want to know more about, there is no faster way to become an expert than to

teach it. You'll find you learn 10 times faster when you're teaching others, and you can do the teaching right over the Internet via webinar, podcasts or even by email. Once you've finished teaching your course, turn your outline and content into an info product, and add the recordings to it for an easy $97 or $197 product.

3. Take Courses. If you're looking for fresh ideas, take a course in your niche and use it as a jumping off point to create your own product.

4. Use Your Life Experience. Did you successfully get your children through the terrible 2's or the dreaded teenage years? Do you have some great advice to offer other parents? Then you've got the makings of a product. Did you lose weight? Did you get in shape? Did you go from deep debt to deep pockets? Life experience can be used to create hot selling products, and because you've lived the information, it's really easy to impart it to others.

5. Write About a Process. Perhaps you built an electrical business from the ground up, or you bought a business and turned it from a losing proposition into a money maker. Or maybe you perfected a process for turning iron into gold. Whatever the process, there is a good chance others are more than happy to learn from your mistakes and take advantage of the many shortcuts you can show them.

6. Write About Your Hobby. If you've got a hobby you love, odds are there are others who love it as well. Do you collect

baseball cards? Do you paint? Do you collect old books? Whatever it is, find a way to use your knowledge to help others with the same interest.

7. Compile Anecdotes or Stories. Choose a common theme, and then compile stories that follow that theme. Think "Chicken Soup for the Soul" and you'll know what I mean. If you're using other people's stories, be sure to get permission. This can be a super fast way to create a product or a book; simply write the intro, choose a catchy title, and compile the stories.

8. Find a Need and Fill It. Ask your readers and customers what they want to know, and create a product that fills that need. For example, one lawyer kept hearing from his business clients that they wished they had an easy reference for business law basics so they wouldn't have to call the lawyer with every question they had. He wrote the product and sold thousands of copies.

9. Narrow Your Niche. Maybe you've already got a topic for your next product, but there are too many competitors selling the same topic. Narrow the focus of your topic so that your angle is different from all the other products. For example, you want to write a book on growing roses, but there are hundreds of books out there already on that topic. Narrow your focus to growing roses on a patio (for apartment dwellers) or growing roses in harsh northern climates and you've probably got a winner.

10. Keep Your Eyes Open and Your Brain Active. Watch for

things that spark your interest and ask lots of questions and you'll find topics everywhere – you just need to learn to spot them. For example, when you're having a conversation or listening to the radio, ask yourself "Where is the product in this?" You'll be surprised by the wide variety of answers you get – often times they're things you normally never would have thought of.

What to Do When Your Product Idea is Already Taken

You've got a DYNAMITE idea for a new product and you can't wait to get started on it – or maybe you already have. Then it happens: You see that someone else has beaten you to the punch and released a very similar product just last week.

Now what should you do??

At this point many people will simply fold. They'll scrap their product idea and begin a search for a new idea.

Then there's the successful marketers who wouldn't bat an eyelash just because someone else released a product like theirs. They would go ahead and finish their product and release it as soon as possible.

Do you know why? Two reasons: First, a successfully selling product on a particular topic means there's room for another product on the same topic. And the reason there's room is because of reason number 2: People who are deeply interested in a topic don't buy just one book or just one course – they buy everything they can get their hands on.

In fact, the person who released their product ahead of yours did you a favor, because you can now see how well their product is selling. You can look for the information holes they forgot to fill and you can be the one to create the better product. You can also see what their price point is and act accordingly. If they're priced at $17, you might want to shoot for a much higher price to convey a much higher value. On the other hand, if they are selling their product at several hundred dollars, you can choose to become the affordable alternative.

So next time you've got a great product idea and someone else beats you to the punch, you might want to thank them.

One more thing – don't be afraid to approach them and ask to do a deal. They might very well be open to being your affiliate and mailing your offer to their list. If your products are very similar, they can mail to their list of non-buyers. If there's a difference such as price, they might mail to their entire list.

Remember – competition can be a GREAT thing when you're marketing online.

5. Social Media Hacks

How to Get People Tweeting About Your Product

Take a lesson from the Kraft marketing handbook, add you own twist and see what happens. Kraft ran a Twitter promotion in which the company identified pairs of people tweeting about Kraft Macaroni and Cheese and then contacted them, awarding prizes to the first to respond. This simple campaign garnered 1.5 MILLION tweets, yet it only cost the company awards of t-shirts and boxes of Mack and Cheese.

Now the company is trying something new: Turning the best Macaroni and Cheese tweets into commercials that run the same evening as the tweets were sent.

And while you might not be ready for prime-time, these ideas can easily be adapted to your own business. In the case of the first campaign, simply offer free downloads to the winners, or physically male them CD's or DVD's.

As to turning tweets into same day ads, why not put the best tweets about your products on the home page of your website and make the tweeters "famous" for a day? You could even incorporate your favorite tweets right into your sales materials, videos and books. Lots of people want to see their name in print, and it will cost you next to nothing to create your own viral tweeting campaigns.

4 YouTube Marketing Mistakes Committed by Internet Marketers

YouTube is a great tool for marketing your business – if you can avoid the pitfalls...

Mistake #1 – Thinking all you need to do is upload a video and traffic will flood your website.

No less than 35 hours of video is uploaded to YouTube every minute, so the competition to get your video seen by viewers is insane. There are tons of high-quality videos that never get more than a few thousand views, and no doubt many more that get even fewer eyeballs.

What to do? First, tailor your video content to what your viewers want and not necessarily to what you want to show them. Always keep the viewer in mind every step of the video making process and put their needs and desires ahead of yours. Next, you've got to vigorously promote your video. Social sites are often the best way to get the word out. And third, realize that it takes time, resources and a good idea to make a video people want to watch and pass on to others. And it takes time and resources to properly promote your video. Don't expect to slap up any old video and watch the sales role in.

Mistake #2 - Thinking you're too small or new to make video work for you and your business.

Just because you need to keep your expectations realistic doesn't mean placing and promoting videos on YouTube can't have an impact on your business. Any business, large or small, can use video to its advantage.

Think about what you like to share with friends and tailor your video accordingly. Even a few thousand views can increase your business, and if you get lucky, you might even create the next video viral sensation.

Mistake #3 - Creating a commercial. Online video is about engagement with others, not slapping out another "buy my product" commercial.

Think of your video as doing much more than simply selling a product or service. People on YouTube want to consume and share engaging and fun content, so don't give them a 30 minute speech on why your product rocks, because odds are they won't watch it.

Instead, inject fun, personality and pizzazz into your videos. Make them emotional, or thought provoking, or funny, or all three. Ask yourself: If I saw this video, would I send it to my friends? If the answer is no, then keep working on your concept.

Another test to see if you're on the right track: If you with friends, would you show them the video? If not, then you might want to start over. A video should grab attention and keep the viewer entranced. It should be short – usually less than 5 minutes and preferably less than

2.5 minutes. And it should leave the viewer feeling GLAD they saw it, not glad it's over.

Mistake #4 - Trying too hard. You might think you need to spend thousands of dollars to get a professional video created, when the fact is an amateur type of video might do just as well, if not better.

People generally don't like "slick" unless it's of a "Hollywood" caliber – and that's expensive. People prefer to watch videos of real people doing real things. To illustrate slick versus real, think of an overly smooth sales person trying to sell you a car – isn't he or she an instant turn off? Now think of an average nice person with a car for sale. She tells you it's a good car, but the heater takes 10 minutes to warm up and the ride's not super smooth. Who do you trust?

Or think about the person trying desperately to impress you with how professional he is and how he knows everything about everything, compared again with the average nice person who readily admits she makes bone-headed mistakes and sometimes says or does the wrong thing. Who do you like better?

Bottom line: Do create videos to market your business on YouTube, don't expect them to get a gazillion views overnight without massive promotion, do be yourself when making the videos, and ALWAYS keep the viewer in mind through every step of the process.

Tricks to Getting Retweeted

When your tweets get retweeted, a whole new group of followers is exposed to your tweet, and thereby you. The more your tweets are retweeted, the greater number of followers who get to see them. Why is this important? Because the added exposure can mean you get new followers as well as more clicks to your website.

So are there any tricks to getting retweeted? Absolutely, and I've picked out some of the best...

1. Write good stuff. Seriously – write tweets that people enjoy, that are interesting or useful or entertaining or helpful. Recall the kinds of things you've retweeted – you don't forward boring stuff, you retweet only the best tweets, and that's what your followers do as well.

2. Anything about Twitter is retweetable. Think about it – what is the ONE thing every single person on Twitter has in common? Twitter! So when you find an article with Twitter tips, or the latest editorial rant on why Twitter is bad, or great, or the marketing bonanza of all time – go ahead and tweet about it.

3. Break news - whether it's a tornado moving through your backyard or the latest development in your niche - tweet about breaking news as soon as you hear about it.

4. Tweet "How-to's." People love tweets that begin with, "How to..." regardless of whether it's how to make sauerkraut chocolate cake, get more done in less time or hot wire a car.

Another phrase that also gets retweeted a lot is "The art of..."

5. Use links in your tweets. Providing a link adds credibility and gives your followers a place to go for more information. Always add a link if it's pertinent.

6. Tweet about the weird, strange and bizarre. Glow in the dark goldfish and naked graffiti artists will get retweeted non-stop for DAYS, so go ahead and tweet about the weird stuff, because you are NOT the only person who loves being surprised and shocked.

7. Which brings us to the last one – be surprising, be different, be FUN. More than almost anything else, people love to be entertained – so go ahead and get a little crazy, let the kid in you shine through, and transmit that innate sense of pleasure in living life to your followers.

Bottom line: The more you get retweeted, the better. And what's the number one trick to getting retweeted? Believe it or not, it's simply ASKING your followers to retweet you.

Is Social Media Gaining You New Customers? Or Just Wasting Your Time?

More and more I'm seeing that there is a "trick" to social media, and it's not to bombard people with a plethora of content. Rather, it's to use specially crafted content designed to lure a customer in and get them at least one step closer to becoming your customer.

Have you ever gone fishing? What's the secret to becoming a great fisherman or fisherwoman? It's not blanketing the water with bait.

Sure the fish will consume it, but if it's got no hook, how are you going to reel them into the boat? Instead, the secret lies in using the right bait on the right hook AND knowing what to do when you get the nibble – that is, setting the hook before the fish gets away.

So what's your bait in social media? It's helping the person to solve a problem. Think about this – you've got a problem and it's causing you stress, perhaps making you lose money, lose sleep, or just plain irritate you. You don't know what to do. You begin searching the Internet for answers, but nothing seems to fit until you run across a person on Facebook / LinkedIn / Twitter, etc. who claims to know something about your challenge. You provide a few details and ask him or her what to do and BOOM! They give you a solution that HOT-DIGGITY-DOG actually WORKS! How do you feel about that person? More to the point, are you open to doing business with that person? If you're like the vast majority, the answer is a resounding "YES!"

So what happens next? If this person is smart, they're going to get you to take another step. It might be to opt into a list, get on a skype call or make a small purchase. They are setting the hook and you are HAPPY to be joining them. Contrast this scenario with one of throwing out a ton of content here there and everywhere and hoping upon hope that somebody somewhere notices and raises their hand and says, "SELL ME SOMETHING, please!" Sure it happens, but it's not a system – it's a crap shoot.

So here is what I propose – become the helpful go-to person in your niche, whatever it might be. Demonstrate that you WANT to answer questions and help people. In fact, use your social media time specifically for this one purpose – answering questions in your niche. On days when no one asks a question, give the answer to a common problem – guaranteed someone out there is searching for a solution to that exact problem the moment you are posting.

By focusing on offering real solutions instead of simply spewing content, you'll find you spend LESS time in social media and get far better results.

Is Your Business Suffering From Abandoned Social Media?

You started that Facebook Page or Twitter account with the best of intentions – but that was 2 years ago and you haven't been active on it for 6 months. Does it matter? In a word, yes.

Let's say a prospect finds your website and likes what they see. They want to hire you or buy your product, but first they want to dig just a little deeper. They find your Twitter profile and see you've sent out 12 tweets in 12 months and you have 22 followers. Are they impressed? No. Odds are you've just lost a customer.

If you have social media accounts or blogs that you aren't using, you've got two options: Either get busy making them active or close them down. An inactive account will hurt you far more than no account at all.

How To Use Bad News For Good

You probably heard about Justine Sacco's twitter message about AIDS that got her fired from her position as communications director for InterActiveCorp. Justine tweeted: "Going to Africa. Hope I don't get AIDS. Just kidding. I'm white!" During her long flight from London to South Africa, a global outcry on Twitter and around the web called for her firing. By the time she landed she was out of a job. You can read the NY Times story here: http://bit.ly/jsacconews

But there's more than one take away here. The first and obvious one is to be careful what you put into social media, because one idiotic message is all it takes to derail your good name and your business.

Second, scroll to the very end of the story and you'll see this:

> *Out of the firestorm came a social good effort. Someone created the website,* http://justinesacco.com *to bring attention to charitable organizations working to battle AIDS.*

What an interesting idea: Turning someone else's bad social media manners into something quite positive. In this case the person who registered the domain chose to remain anonymous, using domains by proxy. But if you're on the lookout for opportunities to turn the latest 'scandal' into something positive and newsworthy - and you do it right - you could generate some positive press and word-of-mouth for your business in the process.

And the third lesson here is of course to purchase your own URL name. Someone could have just as easily turned justinesacco.com into yet another social nightmare for the ex-communications director.

6. Traffic Hacks

Diversification and Differentiation are Keys to Staying Alive

The more dependent you are on one form of traffic, the more vulnerable you are. Just ask those who depended on Google for all their traffic and then got hit in the face with another zoo update. In fact, if you are dependent on one of anything in your business, sooner or later you will be punished for your vulnerability, and this goes double for traffic generation.

"But I don't use Google for traffic, I use referrals, or I use guest blogging, or I use banner ads..." It doesn't matter. If you are using just one source for traffic, then you are one unforeseeable problem away from losing all of your traffic.

Mechanically, every mode of traffic generation can have problems. Logistically, what works today might not work tomorrow. For example, if you have an offline business in the United States and you use radio or television to get traffic to your store, then every four years you'll experience a 3 month period during which the political parties are willing to pay far more than you for ads, and you'll likely lose your ad space. If you depend on joint ventures and referrals, you already know this can run hot and cold. This week you have 3 people sending you traffic, but for the next 4 weeks you've got nothing until you manage to drum something up again. So rule number one of traffic is to get 3 to 5 steady sources of new traffic, new leads, new prospects and new customers.

Rule number two is to differentiate yourself from all the other noise out there. If you go to the Warrior Special Offers forum, what do you find? Essentially, it's a really large Internet Marketing swap meet. Go to a real swap meet and you find all kinds of vendors with all kinds of stuff selling at low prices.

The Warrior Forum is no different, and if you take this one step further you realize that the entire Internet is yet another swap meet on a much larger scale. Every vendor is vying for the attention of the customer, and the customer can go anywhere and buy from anyone or simply watch Netflix instead of reading your sales page.

That's why you've got to find your own special hook that sets you apart from everyone else and essentially puts you in a class of 1 with no competition.

I Don't Want to Pay for Traffic!
This is a common statement from new online marketers - *"I don't want to BUY traffic, I want to get it for free!"* At first glance this sentiment makes sense. After all, why would you pay for traffic if you could get it for free? But the smart marketer - or at least the marketer who knows how to consistently make money - will adamantly disagree. In fact, the most profitable marketers routinely

82

pay for traffic because overall the more they spend, the more they make.

Wouldn't you pay $1 to make $1.50? In fact, wouldn't you do it all day long? Before we go further into paid traffic, let's dispel a common Internet Marketing myth:

If you have a great product, people will find you.

In 99 cases out of 100 that's utter rubbish. Let's say you're selling a product that produces wonderful benefits to the consumer. And you're selling it from inside your bedroom closet, and no one knows about you or your product. How many will you sell?

Building a website and thinking people will magically come is no different than the bedroom closet scenario. No one will stumble on you or find your product unless you go out and bring them back to your house. Yes, there are methods of getting traffic without paying for it up front. For example, affiliate marketing is often touted as being the best way to get free traffic. Of course, you pay in time to recruit the affiliates, and then you pay a high percentage to the affiliates for each sale they make. So while this kind of traffic is excellent, it most definitely is not free.

And it's not repeatable, either. That is, you must continually find new affiliates to promote for you or your sales system sits idle. It's a never ending cycle of recruiting new affiliates, getting their sales and then recruiting more affiliates. The exception? If an affiliate is BUYING traffic to send to your offer. Think about that – if your affiliate is buying traffic, you could do the same thing and keep ALL of the sales instead of splitting it with the affiliate.

And as a side note, affiliate marketing can actually be risky. Many people on some affiliate sites have lost money to scam affiliates. In addition, all it takes is a handful of bad affiliates to send you lousy, non-converting traffic to send your conversion rates down the tube. Now when a good affiliate looks at your stats, they'll think you have an offer that doesn't convert and they won't touch it.

Then there's the 'free' traffic you get from forums, from YouTube, from blogging and so forth. This isn't actually free either because you have to invest your time, effort and skills in getting the 'free' traffic. And there is no guarantee after all of your hard work that the traffic will show up, especially in any real quantity.

Next, there's cheap traffic, also known as junk traffic. Buy 1,000 visitors or 1,000 Likes or 1,000 Tweets and see how much you make. Nothing. In this case, what you have done is waste $5 on Fiverr.

"But If I Have to Buy Traffic, I'll Lose Money"

This might be true if your funnel is non-existent. Let's look at two examples: Joe is selling a $10 ebook. Andrea is also selling a $10 ebook, with a high converting $47 upsell, a second upsell for a $19 a month continuity program, and a third upsell of a $1997 coaching program. In both cases, Joe and Andrea will also market affiliate products to their customers.

Joe's lifetime value of a customer is $10 plus whatever affiliate sales he might make in the future, if any. Andrea's lifetime customer value might easily exceed $100 (depending on how many upsells each customer typically purchases) plus any affiliate sales she makes in the future. $10 versus $100 – who can afford to buy traffic? They both can, but in Joe's case he's going to have to be extremely careful and cautious because he's got very little room for error. He's got to test everything to make sure he's converting at the absolute highest level. And he's got to get just the right traffic in just the right way to his offer that is presented perfectly to each particular traffic stream.

Joe also has to take up meditation to deal with the stress of having such a tiny profit margin. Andrea, on the other hand, has 10 times the profit to work with. So while Joe might only be able to afford to pay a few cents per visitor, Andrea can likely afford to pay several dollars per visitor.

Do you see the difference? If your funnel is set up correctly, you never have to fear buying traffic. The trick is to make the right offers and then buy the right traffic. When you do this, you're set. You're not dependent on organic traffic, on Google search, on affiliates or anything else. You have a stand alone system that works for you day in and day out, and you know that as long as you work the system, the system will continue to pay you.

This is a radical shift in thinking for many marketers who have always focused on getting 'free' traffic. Paradoxically, buying traffic can be an extremely freeing experience. Gone are the days of hoping you persuade a good affiliate to promote you, or hoping that your latest guest post will send a rush of traffic, or hoping that someone "discovers" your product and tells the world.

Yes, you absolutely should still recruit affiliates because they can sometimes bring you huge results. But the difference is you no longer depend on those affiliates – affiliate sales are just icing on your already large triple chocolate cherry cake.

When you use paid traffic, you are in the driver's seat. You determine how much you make. Want to make more? Then you can either improve the conversions on your funnel to sell more people, increase the number of products your customers can purchase, or buy more traffic. Better still, you can do all three.

Use Re-Targeting To Get Visitors To Come Back To Your Website

As marketers we're all familiar with the fact that many visitors don't convert the first time they come to your website. For whatever reason they leave without purchasing your product, even though they might have been keenly interested in buying.

If you do manage to capture their email address, you can continue marketing to them. But what if they don't opt in to your list? Unless you do something, you will likely lose those visitors forever.

That's why retargeting/remarketing is such a great idea. Simply by adding a bit of code to your website, remarketing "tags" place a cookie on your visitors. Now when they leave your website, they see ads that are encouraging them to go back to your website and complete what they started. For example, if you're selling a service, your ads would remind them of your service and clicking your ad will send them straight back to your website.

These ads will give you a much higher conversion rate than normal because the people viewing them have already expressed interest by visiting your website. As most sales people will tell you, often times making the sales is simply a matter of asking for it enough times until you get that yes. And with remarketing your visitors see reminders of you everywhere. Some of those visitors will return and purchase your product, or at the very least opt in to your list.

There are actually different types of remarketing that you can use:

1. Site remarketing is the example above – your ads keep you in their mind after they've left your website.
2. Search remarketing is targeting search engine users who have searched for the keywords of your choice. Choose your search terms wisely, because some searches are much more likely to result in sales than others.
3. Social media remarketing is like site remarketing – you place a bit of code on shared links within social networks and then serve relevant ads. When your link is forwarded, the people receiving the link also see your ads.

What are the biggest benefits to use remarketing? Obviously you stay in front of your visitors after they've left your website. This provides you with a greater return on your traffic – the same traffic yields better results and more sales. Plus you get to try different calls to action. What motivates one person to buy might be different than what motivates someone else. By giving them a variety of marketing messages, the odds increase that one will hit home.

You can even segment your website users based upon specific actions they've taken on your website. Thus they are reminded of the same product they looked at, even if you offer dozens of different possibilities. This is yet another reason why remarketing works so well – you are able to zero in on their exact interest and market to them accordingly.

For more information on remarketing (also known as retargeting) read SEOMOz's great introductory blog post: http://bit.ly/seomoz1

You can also check out the 7 Types of Effective Retargeting from Business to Community: http://bit.ly/7retarg

Or you might read the 6 Types of Retargeting Every Marketer Should Know by Search Engine Watch:

http://bit.ly/6typesretarg

7. Sales Copy Hacks

How to Know if Your Sales Copy Sucks

You've just finished writing the sales copy for your new product. Wouldn't it be great if there was a way to test your copy BEFORE you actually send prospects to it? Because think about this – if you send a 1,000 people to your sales letter and NOBODY buys, you've just wasted all that traffic. And if you spent money to get that traffic, you're out that investment. Even if it was free traffic, you've still burned your chance to sell them on your product. Odds are even if you do rewrite the copy, they're not going to go back a second time and read it again. (Unless you offer some kind of incentive, in which case you might be able to bribe them into taking a second look.)

If only there were a way to know ahead of time whether your copy is good or not... wait, there is!

Here's what to do – turn off the phone, sever your Internet connection and refuse to be distracted for the next hour. Now then, imagine you are the prospect. You are thinking like the prospect, feeling like the prospect, experiencing the same issues, same problems, same questions as you prospect, etc. Put yourself in their shoes and reread your letter from start to finish. Do not spend time making corrections or anything else – simply read the letter as though you are a prospect considering buying this product.

Finished? Now rate how well your copy accomplishes the following, assigning a number 1 - 5 to each element.

1 means "Practically non-existent"

2 is "Room for serious improvement"

3 means "Not horrible, but could be better"

4 is "Strong"

And a 5 indicates "You positively NAILED it."

Ready? Here we go...

1. Does the headline instantly grab your attention? _____
2. Does the lead-in compel you to read further? _____
3. Are the headline and lead-in completely believable? _____
4. Is the headline and lead-in combo likely to resonate powerfully with a significant number of your prospects? _____
5. Does the headline and lead-in combo offer powerful benefits? _____
6. Does the spokesperson establish his/her qualifications beyond doubt? _____
7. Do the emotions you experience while reading the first few paragraphs compel you to want to read further? _____
8. Is the prospect given a reason why he or she must read this, and must read this now? _____
9. Does the copy read like a conversation between two friends? _____
10. Is it clear that the spokesperson truly has the best interests of

the prospect at heart? _____

11. Are the product's benefits fully explored? _____

12. Are the emotional reasons for purchasing fully developed?

_____

13. Does the letter entertain and inform as well as sell? _____

14. Is the price fully justified and trivialized? _____

15. Is the guarantee prominent and does it restate the benefits?

_____

16. Is there a compelling reason why the prospect should immediately make the purchase? _____

17. Is there a sense of urgency? _____

18. Do you feel yourself getting more and more excited as you move through the letter? _____

19. Is the call to action compelling enough that you would feel silly for not ordering immediately? _____

20. Is the prospect told exactly what to do next, how to order and how s/he will receive their product? _____

21. If you were a prospect, would you make the purchase? _____

Scoring

21- 50: Stop right there. Do NOT use this copy until make significant changes.

51 – 65: Not good, but at least you've made a start. Now go back and make the adjustments your letter needs.

66 – 80: Not bad for a draft, but not good enough to use unless you just don't have the time to fix it, OR your offer is so compelling ($100 cars, for example) that it doesn't need a strong letter.

81 – 95: Looking good. A little tweaking here and there can still improve your conversions.

96 - 105: Congratulations! Maybe you should be writing copy for a living!

Just What Is Hype, And How Can You Avoid Using It?

No doubt you've been told to avoid using "hype" in your copywriting and sales messages, right? And I'll bet there have been times when you've closed a sales letter page because the hype was too ridiculous for words. But when it comes to defining hype and especially to determining how much is just right, the water gets murky and no two marketers can give you the same answer.

That's because "hype" is subjective. One prospect's perception of hype is another prospect's perception of just the right sales message to get them to buy. In addition, you need some hype to sell. No hype = no excitement, which means no sale. Here's what I mean:

Sales message example #1: "This system is for sale for $33.33, here's the order button."

Now you've got to admit, that's hype free. It's also benefit free, boring and will capture the interest of just about nobody. Of course, if the system is already well-known and you're discounting it to 5 bucks, you've made a sale. But if you're selling a good product at a reasonable price, you're going to have to turn on the hype. Here goes:

Sales message example #2: "This Revolutionary New System Cuts Your Work in Half While Tripling Your Productivity."

Not bad, and certainly worthy of further investigation if you're interested in getting more work done in less time. And yes, there is hype for sure, especially in the words "revolutionary" and "new" – just not so much that it raises red flags and causes your prospect to tune out.

Sales message example #3: "The Easy System that Earns You a Thousand Dollars a Second with NO Work."

Looking at the words themselves, there isn't much in the way of hype. We didn't say it's the greatest system in the world, or that everyone loves it, or that there's never been anything like it since the beginning of time. However, is it believable? No. And therefore, the promise is just so much hype in the ears of the prospect and doesn't offer enough substance.

Sales Message Example #4: "Give Me 5 Hours and I'll Show You How to Earn $1,439 Per Month on Autopilot."

Hyped? I don't think so. This message offers a specific benefit in exchange for a specified about of work – 5 hours. The amount doesn't sound unreasonable because we've all see examples of a few hours of work resulting in a monthly income of several hundred or even a couple of thousand dollars per month. Most importantly, the reader isn't being promised something for nothing, which will ALWAYS instill doubt in a prospect. It sounds honest, it doesn't sound hyped, and it's completely plausible.

What have we learned from these examples? Plenty. First, if you don't use some hype you're never going to sell much of anything. People need to get excited before they'll whip out their wallets and they need to see a clear benefit to making the purchase. They WANT to be fired up, they want to feel their heart race a bit and experience that adrenaline rush of getting a great deal. The better you can extrapolate how the features of your product will benefit the consumer and improve their life, the more likely they are to click the order button.

Second, be believable. Making wild claims is the ultimate in hype – and if you can't back those claims with rock solid absolute undeniable proof, you're better off not making those claims at all.

Third, be specific. "Make $2,000 a month!" sounds much more like hype than "Earn $2,078.55 a month." Why? Because the specific number is more credible, as though it's already been done. "Type Faster" doesn't mean much, but "Type 15 Words Per Minute Faster after Just 4 Lessons" tells the prospect exactly what to expect. Non-specific claims and rounded numbers just naturally sound like hype, regardless of whether or not they're factual.

Fourth, tell them what the catch is. This goes right back to being believable, because if you tell someone they can get a great benefit, they immediately want to know what the catch is. Often this equates to price, but if you can show a different catch, such as "5 hours," then you take their mind off of price and onto the question of, "What do I need to do for 5 hours to make that $1439 a month?"

And by the way – normally an article like this would start out with the definition of hype, but I wanted to save this gem for the end. Here's what hype really means:

Hype: Verb meaning to stimulate or excite

Hype: Noun meaning extravagant or exaggerated claims

As you can see, hype is good so long as we strive to stimulate and excite, rather than exaggerate or stretch the truth.

Add A Decoy, Make More Sales

In the book, Predictably Irrational, there is an experiment that involved subscriptions to the magazine The Economist. Two groups of subjects were offered two different sets of options. Here they are, with results:

Offer A:

$59 – Internet Only Subscription (68 chose)

$125 – Internet and Print Subscription (32 chose)

Total Sales – **$8,012**

Offer B:

$59 – Internet Only Subscription (16 chose)

$125 – Print Only Subscription (0 chose)

$125 – Internet and Print Subscription (84 chose)

Total Sales – **$11,444**

So what accounted for the higher sales of the more expensive option in Offer B? As you might have guessed, it was the decoy offer of the Print Only Subscription. By offering a similar but inferior option at the same price, sales of the Internet and Print Subscription rose dramatically.

Why? Perhaps because by comparison it looks like such a great deal. And you don't have to make the offers the identical price – you only have to price them closely. For example, if you're offering an information course, you might go with these options:

- Intro Package (Single Component) Instant Download $27
- Entire Package Instant Download $92
- Entire Package Instant Download with Mailed DVD $97

Is the lower priced option necessary? You'll have to test to find out, but I'm betting your overall sales will be higher if you do offer a significantly lower priced option as well.

Increasing Sales By Discovering Your Buyers' Secrets

Like it or not, the balance of power in the marketplace has shifted from sellers to buyers. Buyers have more information at their fingertips and more choices available than ever before. And because of this, if you don't have a good understanding of your customers then your marketing is going to be akin to throwing mud against the wall in the hopes that something, somewhere sticks.

The trick to knowing your customers? It's as simple – and as difficult – as turning halfway around so that rather than viewing your business through your eyes, you're now looking at it through your customers' eyes.

The more attuned you are to seeing your business through your customers' eyes, the more successful you will become. Here then are steps you can take to make this transition...

1) Ask yourself, "What do your customers need?" What is the customer trying to accomplish and how are you going to help them accomplish it? What's the result they're looking for, and why are they going to contact you to get that result?

2) Understand the context in which they're seeing your marketing message. Are they getting input from friends and family? From experts? What websites are they visiting? What kinds of offers are they exposed to?

3) What's important to your customer? What is your buyer thinking, feeling, doing and saying?

4) What's your customers fears? What kind of pain are they in? What keeps them up at night?

5) What are your customers' aspirations and goals? What are they seeking, and what do they want to achieve?

Try to get in their head and speak as they would speak and think as they would think. Rather than saying, "My customer is afraid of losing her husband if she doesn't lose weight," say it from her point of view. "I'm afraid (terrified?) of losing my husband if I don't lose this ugly fat." See the difference? Your goal is to really channel that person and find out what it feels like to be them. As you can imagine, this is going to help you tremendously with your marketing message.

6) How does your customer perceive you, your business and your product? Your customers want to know how your product is going to really help them, if they can trust if you, if they feel comfortable buying from you. Imagine being them: "Is this going to work? Will I get the results I want? "Does this guy know what he's doing?"

7) And now we come to an element almost no marketer thinks about – justification. Your customer may have to justify their purchase to a spouse or boss. They've got to explain their decision. "What am I going to tell my wife? How will I explain to the boss that this is the best choice?"

8) Next – what style of buyer is your typical customer? Are they:

❖ The person who wants to have all the facts and details before they make a decision?

❖ Spontaneous, living in the moment, disliking details, making quick decisions and afraid they'll miss out on something great?

❖ Slow to make decisions, placing others needs ahead of their own, looking at the big picture?

❖ Or are they curious, goal-oriented, highly motivated and focused on doing whatever it takes to be competitive?

9) Once you understand which general type of buyer your customers tend to be, you can personalize your marketing for that particular type of buyer, all the way from how they like to receive their information to how they make that final buying decision.

10) And lastly, where are your customers found? Not only in terms of geographic location, but also in terms of what websites do they frequent, when do they go there, and how can you attract their attention?

The more you can get into your customer's head, the more you can tailor your products and the marketing of those products to exactly suit your customers, the more successful you will be. I simply cannot stress this enough: Buyers hold the cards, and until you learn to sit down at the same table with them and play by their rules, your business won't be nearly as profitable as it could be.

How To Get More Donations – And Sales

If you solicit donations for anything, then you've got to read about Smile Train's 46% increase in fund raising by offering "donate to opt-out." That's right – Smile Train offered donors the chance to make a one time donation in exchange for never being asked to donate again.

In an experiment with their entire list, the once-and-done group donated $260,783, while the standard letter group donated $178,609. Even more interesting, only 39% of those who donated under the once-and-done group actually indicated they wanted no further communications. The rest either wanted to receive limited communications or regular updates.

If you take donations on your blog or website, you might offer your readers the chance to donate once and you will never ask again.

Taking it a step further – how could you apply this to sales? Purchase once and you never purchase again – it could work for a membership site, software, etc.

8. Business Success Hacks

Want To Be An Expert In Your Niche? Here's How:
"I Hereby Dub Thee, Super Duper Pooper Expert! Now Go Forth And Do Business!"

If only it were that easy to become an expert – just get someone to tap a sword on both your shoulders as you kneel and PRESTO! You are the go-to person for your niche. Wait – it actually can be almost that easy.

The first thing you need to know about becoming an expert is WHY you want to be one. When you are viewed as the expert, people want to buy your products and services. They also want to promote you. Whether it's sharing your stuff via social media or interviewing you for the news, you become THE person in your niche that people gravitate to.

The second thing to know is HOW to be seen as an expert, and it works like this: You need to ACT like an expert, THINK like an expert, and SPEAK like an expert. And all three of these will become natural when you believe you are indeed the expert. But what if you don't believe you're an expert? Then start acting like you are and your actions will bring about the belief.

Of course, none of this is of any value if you don't have a clue when it comes to your niche. That's why constant study and practice in your field is essential. You've got to know what you're talking about, and the best way to do that is to learn from others as well as from your own experience.

So how do you get others to view you as the go-to person, the expert they should do business with? Here are 12 methods:

1. Choose your niche carefully. It's much easier to be a great big fish in a small pond than a whale in the ocean. For example, if you want to be a business coach, you've got a ton of competition. But if you coach massage therapists on how to grow their businesses, you can very quickly become a whale of a fish in that particular pond.

2. Act like you have a list of thousands, even when making your

debut blog post. Be a professional from day one by imagining you have thousands of people depending on what you say and do. Sure, the only person reading your blog is your grandma, but keep in mind that's going to change soon. The debut post you write today will eventually be read by hundreds or thousands of people, so make it good.

3. Use a great incentive to build your list from Day 1. Yes, offering to keep them updated on your blogposts will yield you some subscribers, but offering a coveted bribe will get you far more. And if your incentive isn't ready yet, just tell them what it is and that by adding their email you'll send them a copy the moment it's ready.

4. Write a newsletter. Yes, an actual newsletter. And do it weekly. Put it in PDF form so readers can download it. Anything in PDF has a higher perceived value, probably because PDF's are often paid for.

5. Interview experts for your newsletter. When you have an expert interview inside your PDF newsletter, it raises your own perceived stature considerably.

6. Hold webinars. This is less effective in the online marketing niche because it's already done so extensively. But if you are in any other niche, offer to hold webinars and give free teaching. You can make these offers via social media and also to list owners. Your goal is to get in front of and help as many people as possible. Make sure they sign up for the webinar – this allows you to capture their email address. And

if you don't yet have a product of your own to promote, offer individual or group coaching at the end of the webinar. Split proceeds with the list owner (if there is one.)

7. Guest blog. The more high traffic websites you can appear on, the better. Always insert your short bio at the end and offer them your free incentive to click your link.

8. Pay attention to what people ask you – it's important. The questions you receive are a great indication of what's on the minds of your prospects. Find ways to answer those questions in a straight forward manner.

9. Skip the big words. You might think being an expert means using a lot of big words and fancy phrases, but what being an expert really means is have the capability to help others further their goals – no fancy lingo needed.

10. Find your voice and your message and stick to them. You don't need to know everything about everything. What you do need to know is a whole lot about a whole little. Choose your stand on a topic and make your best case – don't try to make everyone else's case as well. For example, if your stand is that massage therapists can do 100% of their own marketing and do it completely through the internet, don't tell them how to hire a marketing agency or place a newspaper ad – tell them how to do their own online marketing. That's it.

11. You don't have to reinvent the wheel. You can if you want to, but you don't have to. You might think that to be an expert

you've got to be constantly thinking up new ways of doing things, but that's not true. 99 times out of 100 it's best to stick with what works. For that 100th time, make sure you test it yourself before advising anyone else to try it.

12. Recycle your content. A blog post can become an article in your newsletter, which can become the content for your latest video, etc.

Remember: When you think, act and speak like an expert and have the knowledge to back it up, you ARE the expert. It really is that simple.

13 Proven Tests for Selecting A Profitable Niche

Niche selection is not easy for many. There are a multitude of niches out there both profitable and not so profitable. Test your niche against the following 13 questions to determine if it has profitability potential. If the niche you are looking at passes 9 or 10 of these then it has profitability potential and worth getting into. Passing means getting a Yes for each test question. (click here to be emailed a printable version of this checklist)

1. Does PLR exist in the niche/sub-niche? (Yes/No)

Private Label Rights (PLR) is content that you buy and claim authorship. PLR can be in the form of articles, videos or ebooks. Existence of PLR indicates two things: (1) that people are interested in this niche and (2) you can use the PLR material in marketing or in your niche. When you use it in your niche it is best to add your own ideas/thoughts into it to make it unique. For instance, you can give it a new heading or develop an infograph based on the PLR content. Again if the PLR content is articles only you can develop videos that use these content. Below are great sites that you can buy PLR from:

http://theplrstore.com

http://unstoppableplr.com

http://plrminimart.com

2. Will you be interested in this niche in the long term? (Yes/No)

Is the niche you are interested in one that you have a passion for and will therefore sustain your interest for at least 2-3 years? Granted that the goal is to make money but you have to make money doing what you love and enjoy. The niche has to be one that you will look forward to working in everyday.

3. Is there an existing problem in the niche? (Yes/No)

Niches like self-help, health, weight loss, make money, debt elimination, dating among others are very profitable since people in these niches have an urgent pain/problem that needs to be solved. Does the niche you are researching have inherent pain and urgency?

4. Do ads exist for your niche? (Yes/No)

If you see paid per click (PPC) ads for your main keyword in the search engines its an indication that consumers in that niche spend money. This is a good thing. Naturally the first step is for you to determine your main keyword. For instance, if you plan on helping people make money online, your primary keyword may be "how to make money online" or "make money online". Go to Yahoo.com and do a search for your main keyword. Observe if there are ads with your main keyword on the right hand side or above the regular search results. If there are then this is a good indicator.

5. Does free information exist in your niche? (Yes/No)

The more free information there is in your niche the better since it becomes harder to find good, well organized and high quality information. People will be willing to pay to have well organized and written information in your niche. Do a search in google and find out if people are offering free information in your desired niche. If you see several free information then there is potential to create a profitable information product.

6. Are there Clickbank/Jvoo products in your niche?(Yes/No)

Clickbank (www.clickbank.com) is the largest marketplace for digital products. If there are various digital products in your niche then it's a very good thing. Competition is a very good thing online because it means that people are making money in that particular niche. The more competitors there are the more potential affiliates will be availabe. When you go to clickbank.com, click on affiliate marketplace link at the top and then in the page that displays do a product search using your main keyword. Alternatively, you can also select your niche category in the categories section that is on the left.

Once you select a category, the products in this category will display.

7. Does a forum exist in your niche? (Yes/No)

When a forum or sub-forum exists for your niche then it indicates that this is an area that people are passionate about. To find out if there is a forum in your niche, you can do any of the following:

- Do a google search for your keyword + message board (for example: make money online message board)

- Do a google search for your keyword + "powered by vbullletin" (for example: make money powered by vbulletin)

- Go to http://answers.yahoo.com and search for your main keyword. Observe if people are asking and answering questions in your niche. If you notice common questions, you could answer these in your product.

8. Are there books/magazines in your niche? (Yes/No)

Aside from availability of digital products in your niche, if there are physical books, magazines, or any other non-digital programs in your niche, this is also a good sign that there is proven potential for profit in your niche. To find out if there are non-digital books go to Amazon.com or barnesandnoble.com and search for books that have your main keyword. Additionally, does a "For Dummies" book exist in your niche. The Dummies company does extensive market research before writing books. And so if a "For Dummies" book exists in your niche it is definitely a niche with profit potential. Go to http://www.dummies.com and review the category list or do a search for your niche to find out if a "For Dummies" book exists in your niche.

9. Do experts or gurus exist in your niche? (Yes/No)

If experts/gurus exist in your niche it's a very good thing since you can partner with them in future. For instance, you can interview them by asking them to reveal all their secrets to success in that niche. Then package and sell this interview. For instance, you can have an interview with expert X on how to make money online (use your niche topic here). Perform a google search for your primary keyword and observe if there are any blogs or expert sites that come up on the first 2 pages. Go to the forum in your niche and start a post that asks who the experts in the niche are.

10. Is the niche evergreen? (Yes/No)

An evergreen niche is one that has continuous demand. That is, there are always new prospects looking to buy in your niche. Examples of evergreen niches are weight loss, dating, debt elimination and recovery, investing, stop smoking, etc. The question you should ask yourself is this: "Will there always be new buyers coming into your niche in the near future?"

11. Does it require specialized skills or will it be easy for you to become an expert? (Yes/No)

Is the niche something you can learn and become knowledgeable in or will it require special skill that you will never be good at? It is easy to become knowledgeable in some niches than others. For instance, if you want to teach people how to play guitar and you are not a musician then you will struggle with this. Granted that you can outsource the material on how to do this but you will not be able to provide valuable nuances on guitar playing. On the other hand with adequate research you can learn how to help women overcome menopause symptoms even if you are a man. The fastest way to become an expert in a niche is to buy the top 10 or 20 books in your niche and read them.

12. Will you be able to create multiple products in the niche? (Yes/No)

Its beneficial to have multiple products within your niche with each product solving a specific issue. Each product will be priced differently. A vast selection of products demonstrates that you are an expert in the niche. Additionally, you will easily be able to cross sell your products. You can have a short report, an intermediate course and then an advanced course. Put another way, in the niche you are interested in will you be able to develop a sales funnel? A sales funnel comprises of different products offered at different price points and follow each other sequentially. So once a buyer has purchased your initial $7 product they will be presented with a higher priced product. If they do not buy this then the sale process ends and they are get the $7 they had purchased.

13. Is there opportunity to offer a high ticket product? (Yes/No)

This is not critical but it will be very profitable to have high ticket opportunities in your niche. The various high ticket products are: coaching, boot camps, retreats, seminars. These high ticket product opportunities exist in the weight loss, make money, health, personal development and dating niches. Existence of the possibility of a high ticket product in your niche is an absolute bonus though it is not mandatory.

9 Tips for Better Business Blogging

Blogging can be a great way to position yourself as an authority and create customer loyalty – if you're willing to devote the time necessary.

1. Forgo the advertorial dribble. Decades ago some bright entrepreneur realized that if he wrote his sales copy to look like an editorial, he'd get more readers and more sales. Thus we entered into the age of the "advertorial," and it still works in print publications. Where it does NOT work well is on your blog.

Yes, by all means advertise your products and services on your website, but don't be devious about it. Don't make it look like an article when it's really a self-promotion – it annoys your readers and makes them feel let down when you've got them thinking they're going to learn something new, only to discover they've got to pay to get it.

Thus, do not title your blog post, "Revealed: 35 Ways to Drive Traffic" and then reveal nothing about driving traffic except the order link to your new product. Instead, title your blog post, "Revealed: 5 Ways to Drive Traffic," and then GIVE them the 5 ways. At the end, let them know that if they're interested, you reveal 30 additional methods inside your product and give them the link. They'll respect you for this, and because you've given them good information and demonstrated that you know what you're talking about, it will actually INCREASE your sales.

2. Be the authority. This goes along with Tip #1, because when you're dishing about all the latest updates in your industry rather than spending all your time promoting yourself, you become the expert in your prospects' eyes. And who do people want to do business with? The expert. Who can charge more for their products and services? Again, the expert. Offer up the latest news along with plenty of how-to articles and your readers will come to like and trust you, and thus want to do business with you.

3. Educate, inform and inspire. Whenever possible, use real life stories to inspire your readers. Nothing sells like success, and people love to read how others have overcome the same challenges they're having. Whenever you're stuck for a blog post idea, just think, "What do my readers want to know? How can I help my readers and give them value?" Watch the forums for questions that pop up – this is an excellent source

for ideas.

4. Show your personality. Building reader loyalty takes time and more than just great information – it also takes personality. Let your own unique style shine through in your posts, and don't be afraid to reveal insights about yourself, and to even be controversial when it's called for. Nothing rallies readers like a good controversy, and nothing makes readers more loyal than if they know you well enough to think of you as a friend.

5. Promote your blog. It would be great if you could write it and people would come, but it's seldom that easy. Use your own network to promote your blog by letting them know each time you've made a new post. Guest write for other blogs to promote your own blog. And always ask people to share your blog with others.

6. Ask readers to reply. The more active your blog is, the more appealing it is to new and old readers alike. Always ask your readers to leave their comments on each of your blog posts. You might even consider running a contest to see who can write the best response, and give a prize to the winner.

Whatever it takes to increase comments is something you should consider. Not only does it make your blog appear that much more active and universally liked – it also provides a sense of ownership to each person who takes the time to leave a comment. The more they comment, the more likely they are to tell others about your blog and to return to your blog in the future. And be sure to respond to your reader's comments so they know they're being heard and appreciated.

7. Don't blog unless you really want to. Blogging is a commitment, and while it might seem exciting and fun in the beginning, writing a new blog post every day or two can get old, especially after the first couple of weeks when you feel like nobody's been reading it. If you're not sure you can keep a blog rolling, consider writing guest posts for other blogs, websites and email newsletters. Every publisher is looking for new material, and being the guest blogger or writer puts you in front of an entirely new audience of prospects each time.

8. If you're guest blogging, write a GREAT resources box. Offer them something intriguing with tremendous value for going to your site, and then deliver above and beyond their expectations. This is an excellent method of increasing your list of prospects and becoming well known in your niche.

9. Interview the big dogs. Interviewing others in your niche not only produces great content – it also provides you with powerful contacts and access to their readers when they mention the interview to their own people. So go ahead and ask others in your niche for interviews – the worst they can do is say no, and you'll be surprised how many quickly say yes. Remember, they want to increase their own readership as well, and it's a tremendous ego boost to be sought out and

interviewed as an expert in their industry.

If there is a tip #10, it is this: Have fun. Whatever it takes to make your blog writing fun is what you should do, since your enjoyment and passion for your topic will shine through in your posts. The more fun you're having writing your blog, the more enjoyable it will be for readers to visit and linger.

So yes, have a blast, add humor, don't be afraid to hold yourself up as an example to your readers, (both good and bad,) put your heart and soul into it, and go for it!

5 Methods For Getting TONS of Comments on Your Blog Posts...

You've got traffic, you create great blog posts – and yet only a handful of people bother to comment. Frustrating, isn't it? You work hard to make a great blog post with lots of information your readers can use, but it feels like nobody cares. Worse yet, your blog has the appearance of a ghost town. After all, the more comments your posts receive, the more popular your blog appears. And let's face it, everyone wants to be part of something BIG, something that others are involved with.

So how do you get more replies to your blog posts? And for that matter, how do you get people to reply to your pre-product-launch posts and videos? Here are 5 methods I've found that work...

1) Ask them. That's right – sometimes it can be as simple as asking them to take the action. Ask them to respond to your

post or to a specific question you place at the end of the post. Don't make it a difficult question; Asking whether they prefer chunky peanut butter or smooth peanut butter will pull far more responses than asking how to achieve world peace. (I'm exaggerating the point here, but you get my meaning.)

2) Bribe them. Offer them one of your paid products for free when they leave a comment. You can either give the product to everyone who comments, or to the best comment, or 5 comments chosen at random, etc. Choose a product that your readers are likely to want, and if you're awarding the bribe to everyone, be sure to send it within 24 hours of their posted comment. If you're awarding it to the best comment(s) or to several comments at random, post the winners on your site so that a) your readers know you really gave away the prize and b) it becomes an incentive for them to post a reply to your next blog entry. After all, if someone else won last time, they'll be thinking they've got a shot at winning this time.

3) Make it a contest. Again, you're offering a bribe, only this time it's monetary. For example, offer $100 to the poster who provides the most innovative answer to your question, or to the one who gives the funniest response, etc. Either you can choose the winner, or you can let your readers vote and choose the winner for you. (HINT: This method is also a great way to find out what your reader's biggest challenges are – thus giving you great ideas for new products your readers WANT to purchase.)

4) Give away the launch. If you're launching a new product, give away copies of your new product to the best replies to your post and videos, as well as to random posters. This way you get both the posts that take an effort, and the quickie posts from those who don't want to take a lot of time posting a well thought out answer. This will increase the excitement, increase the exposure of your launch, and can result in some pre-launch testimonials from those who won the product.

5) Be controversial. Taking on topics that hold any kind of controversy will almost always get people talking. People love to take sides, express their opinions, and even get into a discussion. Watch for topics in your niche that spark definite opinions and blog about those – and the replies will naturally come.

6) BONUS Method: While you're giving rewards out, don't limit yourself to replies to your posts and videos. Also reward your readers for re-tweeting your content, telling others, referring others, etc. People will jump through hoops for you if you...

    a) Are offering great content

    b) Make it easy to jump through hoops for you and

    c) You reward them for jumping!

Bottom Line: It's a matter of training your readers to reply to your posts. The more you work to encourage their participation, the more it will become a habit for them to reply. Also take note of which threads tend to get the most response – these are topics that hit hot buttons, and you might want to blog about them more often.

The Best 10 Life Changing Internet Marketing Quotes of All Time

I recently stumbled upon a blog I highly recommend you visit anytime you need a recharge, called http://www.wakeupcloud.com. It's written by a fellow named Henri Junttila, and frankly it's a much needed breath of fresh air in the field of positive self-change.

One of his blog posts is his own personal compilation of "77 Great Quotes That Will Change Your Life," and within that post I discovered 10 quotes that are especially relevant to the of Internet Marketing. I offer them here, along with my personal thoughts. Enjoy!

(a) "If we're growing, we're always going to be out of our comfort zone." John Maxwell

Every first step you take in your Internet marketing career – be it setting up a website, making a blog post, creating a product, doing a launch and so forth – will take you out of your comfort zone. Relish the experience because it means that you are growing, that you are succeeding, that you are LIVING. This applies to building any offline business as well.

(b) "If you wait to do everything until you're sure it's right, you'll probably never do much of anything." Win Borden

Time and time again I see new marketers who are waiting for just the right time to launch a product, just the right moment when they know everything to start a website, just the right alignment of the planets to build a membership site. You'll never know everything you need to know – so just take action. It's like riding a bull – you don't know how he'll try to buck you off, so get on, hang tough, and enjoy the ride. Afterward you'll bask in the glory of your success and plan your next conquest, while those who were too timid will forever wait for the "perfect" time.

(c) "Motivation is what gets you started. Habit is what keeps you going." Jim Rohn

Many people start things in Internet Marketing, but few finish. They start a blog, write a half dozen posts and then quit. They begin creating a product, get halfway finished and then set it aside to go do something else. Others don't even get started because they're too busy bouncing from one idea to the next, never settling on one long enough to begin, much less seeing it through to completion.

So get started, and then keep going. Each day do something - anything that moves you forward. I don't care if it's late at night and you're dead tired – if you haven't moved your business forward today, then DO SOMETHING before you fall asleep. This habit will be the one that propels you beyond the finish line and into the waiting arms of triumph. Remember: If you fail to persist, then you fail.

(d) "Action will remove the doubt that theory cannot solve."
Petryl Hsieh

New marketers doubt their ability, doubt their market, doubt their systems and even doubt their own minds. They doubt their ability to sell, their ability to communicate and I suspect their ability to get out of bed and take action. Result? They buy more ebooks on how to market. They do more reading, more research and more learning, thinking this will remove the doubt and replace it with unbridled confidence.

Reality check – this NEVER works. The ONLY thing that removes doubt and instills confidence is ACTION. All the knowledge, learning and theory in the world cannot erase doubt because it is only through action that anything real is achieved. And without achievement, there is no sense of self worth, and without self worth there is no confidence - only doubt.

Here's an example taken to the ridiculous: A new, intelligent marketer studies how to make a product that everyone will adore. He studies the other products in his market, he studies the market itself, and he works for years at devising the perfect product, which of course has evolved over and over again to adapt to the ever changing market.

While this is going on, a not-so-bright marketer finds a question on a forum about a problem someone has, creates a 20 page report that holds a solution to that problem, and sells it for $7. He sells a couple of hundred copies, which means he now has a list of buyers, $1400 or so in cash and some real world experience in marketing.

The not-so-bright marketer isn't smart enough to know that $1400 isn't a fantastic start. After all, don't those guru websites say you should be making $30,000 your first month? But this guy isn't bright, so he duplicates his efforts and creates more products to sell. Some of these products bomb terribly, some of them do well, and eventually after taking one action after another after another, he has a thriving business and a six figure income.

If only he had been smart enough to know that you cannot create a new product until you know everything there is to know about making and marketing the product, he would surely have been all the wiser and very much the poorer, just like our "intelligent" marketer who knew better.

Too silly? Not really – I see this happen all the time.

(e) "That some achieve great success is proof to all that others can achieve it as well." – Abraham Lincoln

Really, what more is there to say? You've seen other marketers go from homeless or jobless to six figures. This doesn't make them super smart, super special or even super nice. What it does make them is super confident that they can grow their businesses even bigger, larger and more profitable if they choose to – or they can work less and be content with six figures, which is still plenty enough to take tropical vacations and look good in a new car every couple of years.

And since they're not super smart, special or gifted, this should ring one thing loud and clear in your mind and heart – if they can do it, YOU can do it. Period. You might want to make that your mantra – "If They Can Do It, You Can Do It." Say it a hundred times a day if that's what it takes to embed it so deep within yourself that you believe it with every fiber of your being. Because you know what? It's a Fact. Pure and simple. If they can do it, YOU can do it.

(f) "Everyone who got where he is has had to begin where he was." – Robert Louis Stevenson

Funny thing about Internet marketing – there are no prerequisites like there are for being a doctor or a lawyer. No one is going to ask for your credentials before they allow you to become successful. So whether you're a corporate CEO who just got downsized, or someone who's living in his car, it just doesn't matter. Begin where you are right now, with whatever talents you already possess, and build on what you've got.

(g) "Fall seven times, Stand up eight." – Japanese Proverb

The bad news is, you're going to screw up. You're going to make mistakes. You're going to have days that make you wonder if you should quit. That's okay. Pick yourself up one more time, dust yourself off, have a laugh at the situation, and keep going.

When I was new I asked a big time guru to promote one of my products for me. Much to my shock he said yes, and he emailed his entire list. He sent so much traffic to my website that my server crashed within minutes. Can you imagine how mad he was that I hadn't prepared for the avalanche of traffic he sent me? I got my website back up within 2 hours and offered him numerous humble apologies, but he never mailed for me again. Some might have thrown in the towel at that point – heaven knows the thought occurred to me. But I pressed on, and in the grand scheme of things that seemingly horrible, tragic day was but a tiny blip on the screen of life.

What if I hadn't gotten back up? Then you wouldn't be reading these words right now, and I'd be back where I was, wondering what would have happened if only I'd persevered and kept going.

(h) "The path to success is to take massive, determined action." – Tony Robbins

Sure, you can set up a website and hope someday someone comes along and buys your product. Or you can take massive, determined action to drive hordes of traffic to your site. You can hide in the shadows, or you can build a name for yourself and a brand that is recognized the world over. You can write content to try to please everyone, thereby pleasing no one, or you can take a stand and thus stand head and shoulders above the rest.

Taking action is not enough to ensure your success – you must take real, decisive action on a large scale to win the day. Yes it's scary – but it's that leap of faith that can produce remarkable results in a very short amount of time.

(i) **"Always bear in mind that your own resolution to succeed is more important than any other" – Abraham Lincoln**

There will be those who tell you that you can't. That you will fail. That it's a dumb idea, that you don't know what you're doing, that if it were possible, everyone would be doing it. Believe me, there are a thousand ways people can tell you they don't believe in you, but there is only one person's opinion that matters – yours. Resolve to succeed and hold fast to that resolution no matter what happens, and it will simply be a matter of time before you persevere and win the day.

(j) **"He who is not courageous enough to take risks will accomplish nothing in life." – Muhammed Ali**

Remember, courage is not the absence of fear – courage is action in the face of fear. Whatever your fears might be, simply acknowledge them and then move past them. Do not dwell on them, do not make them larger than life, and never allow them to cause you future regret for your inaction.

Fear is almost always an illusion, a simple trick of the mind with no basis in reality. Unless your life is in immediate and real danger, fear is a cosmic hoax perpetrated by the primitive part of your brain that couldn't distinguish an ebook from a duck. All it knows is survival, and really – how many people have died from building websites, creating products or hitting the send button on their email program?

The brilliant thing about Internet Marketing is that there is very little risk other than your time. There's no remortgaging your home to buy web hosting and there's no chance of building a website so shoddy it collapses and crushes you to death. Yet time and again I see people held prisoner by their fear, and nothing makes fear stronger than a lack of action. So anytime you feel fear tingling your spine, take swift, decisive action and you'll be pleasantly shocked at how fast and how far fear retreats back into the shadows.

By now you should have noticed one major theme running through all of these quotes. If you haven't, then I encourage you to go back and figure out what it is, because when you do, success can be yours faster than you ever imagined possible.

How to Steal Your Competitor's Customers
So you would love to nab customers from your competition, but you're finding that it's not easy to change their buying habits. What to do? This fun video might provide a clue...Using the video as inspiration, here are 3 ways to change customer buying habits and swing them over to your business...

Make Change Fun: Changing your customer's buying habits becomes much easier when you can make the process enjoyable. For example, instead of placing your free report on an ordinary white background, use lots of color and shapes like I do in this newsletter to make it stand apart from the crowd. Instead of recording boring talking head videos or screen capture Camtasia videos, go out in the real world and record videos in unusual places with interesting backgrounds and life happening all around you.

Be playful, be different, and engage your customer every step of the way. The more fun it is for prospects to receive your marketing messages and use your products and services, the easier it will be to not only lure them away from the competition, but also keep them coming back to you time and time again.

Be Surprising: A good surprise is fun, pleasant and engaging. It captures interest and holds attention. Research shows that unpredictability activates the part of the brain that anticipates rewards and pleasure, thereby not only getting their attention, but also priming them to expect pleasure from what comes next.

Use Social Validation: There's nothing like happy people already patronizing you to induce more people to do the same. If you want to move a herd of cows, you only need to lead a couple of cows and the rest will follow. And if you want to influence a group of people, you simply show them how much fun or how many rewards a few of them are receiving by patronizing you to get the rest of them to jump in as well. After all, who wants to miss out on all the fun?

Next time you want to change the buying habits of your competitor's customers, trying using the elements of fun, surprise and social validation, and you might be surprised at how many rush to join you.

Are You Repelling Prospects? Good!

A hundred years ago a shop might have tried to be many things to most people. In fact, big box stores still do that today, with good success. Walmart is everything and all things to those looking for the cheapest price. But even they repel customers – namely those people who value service and quality over price.

These days it pays to specialize. Rather than trying to be most things to most people, you want to do one thing and do it really, really well. If you teach gardening techniques, rather than teaching everything to every gardener, pick a focus such as organic vegetable gardening. If you teach marketing, teach it to a very specific audiences, such as chiropractors or coffee shops or contractors.

Yes, you'll be repelling the vast majority of customers, but you'll also be attracting the exact prospects you can help the most. And in so doing, you can also charge accordingly. After all, who commands the highest price – the person who teaches generic marketing techniques to anyone and everyone? Or the specialist who teaches plumbers to build their businesses to seven figures? Every time, it will be the specialist. If you don't believe it, look at the health care industry, one of the biggest businesses of all. Who makes more – a general practitioner or a heart surgeon? Specializing pays, and it pays big.

One more benefit of specializing and perhaps the most important of all is this: You become the only choice. When a dentist wants advice on building his practice and he's faced with 10 choices – 9 of whom do marketing for any kind of business and 1 who works exclusively with dentists, there simply is no competition. Even if your prices are double or triple of your so called competitors, because you are the specialist you will win the business nearly every time and almost without trying.

Bottom line: Know exactly who your target audience is, become their only choice, and repel everyone else who is not a good fit. You'll attract better customers who appreciate you more and are happy to pay for your specialized service and products.

Are Webinars For You?

Perhaps one of the easiest ways to make good money online is by doing webinars. Here's how it works in a nutshell: You choose a date and topic for your webinar, promote it, give great information on the webinar and then promote a product at the end. It's like one big informational sales letter, in that you begin by giving away a great deal of awesome info, and you close by offering them even more information or a service or membership they can use to implement what they've just learned.

If you either have a skill that others want to learn, or you can interview an expert who has the skill people want to learn, the you can do a webinar.

Here are the steps to ensure your webinars generate income...

a) Make the webinar an experience. There is so much I can say about this, but it might all boil down to the following: Do NOT be boring. As you put your webinar together, think about your customers and what they want to learn and experience. Make it interesting, exciting and fun. Plan to show major enthusiasm for your topic, and to answer questions. Remember, they can leave the webinar any time they like, so make sure it's worth staying for.

b) Provide great tools. If you're partnering or using affiliates, provide great blog posts and emails so they can drive as much traffic as possible to your opt-in page. And provide a good variety – you don't want every affiliate sending out the same email, since they begin to look like spam. Instead, consider helping each affiliate to write a unique email tailored exclusively for their list.

c) Spend time on your registration page. This is the page you and your partners or affiliates will be sending traffic to, and it's do or die. Prospects decide whether or not to sign up for your webinar based upon what's on the page, so spend a little time fine tuning it to produce the most sign-ups possible.

d) In creating the slides for your webinar, try to have a new slide every minute or two with one or more important points on it. This keeps the webinar moving and interesting.

e) You can do the webinar by yourself or with a partner. The nice thing about having a partner is you can have a give and take of information, adding in bits that the other might overlook. Of course whoever the expert is will do most of the talking, but the second person can ask questions and add a different dynamic to the call.

f) Promote the webinar. Begin promoting no more than a week in advance because frankly, people have short memories. And as the webinar gets closer, promote it more often with increased urgency.

g) Send reminders. The day before the webinar is the time to send the first reminder, preferably in the early evening. Send the second on the morning of the webinar, and the third reminder 30 minutes before it begins. "Did you forget?" Is a great subject line for the last minute email you send out. Also remind them that there are far more people signed up than there are open webinar slots (assuming this is true, which it usually is.) Suggest they get on the webinar early to ensure they get a "seat."

h) Start the webinar on time. Don't wait for stragglers, you'll just irritate those who bothered to show up on time.

i) Give some of your best stuff. Seriously, you want to majorly over deliver, because the more you give, the more your listeners will want to know. If you hold everything back then not only do you run out of things to talk about – your listeners also wonder if you know anything at all.

j) Be a tease. Seriously, while you're delivering great content you will also be inserting teasers here and there for the pitch that comes at the end. For example, you're telling them how to do "a, b and c," and of course they'll need "d, e and f" which you don't have time to cover here but you'll give them a chance to learn all about it at the end of the presentation. For example: Your webinar is on traffic, so you teach several basic methods on the call and allude to the many advanced techniques they can also use – when they know how.

k) Remember, it's not about you, it's about your audience. If your webinar system allows questions to be typed in (such as GoToWebinar) then the person who isn't doing the talking can keep track of the questions and make sure they get answered. Great trick: Imagine you are a new listener hearing you for the first time. What do you want to know? What isn't clear? What questions might you have? Always keep your listeners in mind, and even periodically check in with them to see if they're following what you're teaching.

l) Make your offer deliciously irresistible. The entire webinar should flow nicely into the offer you're making, and the offer itself should be as irresistible as possible. Pile on the benefits, make it clear what this will allow them to accomplish, and back it with a super strong guarantee. Place the URL of the order page on the screen and tell them exactly what will happen when they order.

m) Give a bonus to the first "x" number who grab your offer. This is a great way to get them off the fence and moving fast. Depending on the price point and the number of listeners, limit your special bonus to the first 10 to 50 people who sign up.

n) Stay on to answer questions and give order updates. If one person has a question there's a good chance others have the same question. Plus you can be there in case they have a problem ordering. And as the orders come in, update the listeners on how many of the bonuses are already gone. This provides proof that others are buying and they should as well. You might even close out the webinar by letting them know you're confident the bonuses will sell out this evening.

o) Follow-up. Send an email thanking them for attending and reminding them of the URL to order if they haven't already.

p) Post the replay online for a few days and inform all those who did not attend to listen to it before you take it down.

It's fairly common to make several thousand dollars from one webinar, depending of course on your offer and your listeners.

What if you don't have a product to promote? Then you've got a couple of options:

1. Choose an affiliate product and ask the product owner to do the webinar with you, splitting the profit between the two of you.

2. Make your product a series of teaching webinars. These are additional webinars that they pay to attend to learn the rest of what it is you're teaching. Record them and get transcriptions, and now you've got a product you can sell on future webinars.

How (And Why) To Build Trust

You've worked hard (darn hard, in many cases) to get prospects to your website and your sales pages – and many times they are on the verge of buying when they suddenly decide NOT to. What happened? How can you get so very close to making a sale only to lose it?

It's no secret that most people are shy about spending money. They've had one or a thousand and one experiences in the past that taught them to exercise massive caution before parting with their hard earned money. For example, they've made a purchase and then never used the product. Or they made a purchase and then realized they had to invest even more money to enjoy the product. Or perhaps they got something for free which ended up costing them time and even money. We've all been there, and the accumulation of those experiences teaches everyone of us to exercise extreme caution when making a purchase, and even when accepting something for free.

Many times the prospect is sitting on the fence, and the result could go either way with the slightest bit of a push. Here are several methods to get more of them to jump off that fence and buy your product. And while none of these are all that glamorous, they are deadly effective at increasing your sales, both short term and long term.

a) Provide lots of detailed, authentic contact information and proof that you are who you say you are. Give your real address and a real phone number. If you have an actual brick and mortar business, regardless of whether or not it is open to the public, show a photo of it. Use photos of yourself and those who work for you on your contact page. Have a group photo of all of you if possible. If you're a solo online marketer, show a photo of you and your family. (Yes, you'll still look professional.) Show photos of yourself at events related to your niche. If you've personally won awards for work in your niche, display those as well.

b) Legitimize your website. Join the Better Business Bureau and display their logo on your website. Display anti-hacker seals on your shopping cart. Has your website won awards? Display them. Do other well-known companies or websites recommend you and your website? Display these seals or recommendations prominently.

c) Make a list of frequently asked questions with detailed answers and display it on your website. Add to the list as you receive questions from prospects and customers.

d) Be consistent. Discrepancies are big red flashing warning signs to prospects and will derail a sale nearly every time.

e) Be honest. Don't just tell them what's so darn great about your product, also tell them what you're product doesn't do or who should not buy it. Be candid, be open, and be real. If you come across as a trusted adviser who always speaks the truth rather than a slick salesman, you will build a loyal customer base who believes what you say and acts on your recommendations with little hesitation. Just as in the offline world, your reputation means everything.

f) Solicit and use testimonials. Never underestimate the power of testimonials. Ask your customers for feedback on the product they purchase and their experience with you and / or your company. Put up a wall of testimonials and place the link to that page on every other page of your website. And don't just use the "Everything was super fantastic!" testimonials. When a customer has a problem, bend over backwards to make it right, and then ask that customer to write about their experience. Everyone knows that even with the best of companies things can go wrong – what they want to know is if you stand behind your business and fix problems when they occur.

g) Ask others to evaluate your website. Find people who aren't afraid to give you the unvarnished truth, and ask them to go over your website just as if they found it through Google or some other means. Ask them how your website makes them feel about your company, what's missing and what can be improved. If they were in the market for your product or service, would they buy? Why or why not? What would make them hesitate? What makes them suspicious or leery? What makes them feel comfortable?

All of these things may seem small and mundane, but you'd be surprised how often they make the difference between getting the sale or losing the prospect forever. ***PS! Thanks for reading thus far. I very much value your time and input. Please leave a review for this book in Amazon.***

The Four Steps to Success

I love it when things are broken down to their simplest, clearest essence, don't you? That's why I was pondering if I could break down what it takes to be successful in just a few words. Not all the books upon books of information, but rather the very essence of what it takes to find success in whatever you choose to do.

Because once you've grasped the essence of something, it becomes a part of you. It's yours – and no one can take it away.

So after much thought, I've come to the following conclusion concerning success...

I believe the consistent, planned achievement of success can be boiled down to doing just 4 things:

1. **Committing to Your Goal**
2. **Setting Up Your Step-by-Step Plan for Reaching That Goal**

3. **Taking Action EVERY Day**

4. **And Then Letting Go of The Outcome**

That's it. No matter what your aspirations are, I believe if you simply and consistently do those four things, you will be successful. Let's take a look at these in order.

First, you've got to have a goal. You can't get to your destination if you don't know what your destination is – how would you know when you've arrived? So you've got to choose a goal, preferable one that makes your heart beat a little faster and puts a smile on your face just thinking about it. You've got to be able to see yourself having achieved that goal. You've got to feel it, believe it and live it even before you take the first step towards achieving it.

But having the goal is not enough – you've also got to be COMMITTED to achieving that goal. This means a complete willingness to do whatever it takes in terms of time, focus, effort and priority. You've got to be determined, not just at the beginning, but all the way through until you achieve your goal.

Second, you need a step-by-step plan for reaching your goal. It's one thing to say you're going to become a millionaire – it's an entirely different thing to actually have a workable plan that will get you there. Chance won't take you there. Sitting and wishing won't take you there. Only by following your plan can you arrive at your destination.

And while it's true there will be roadblocks and detours along the way, you will also find serendipitous good fortune as well, the kind that places the right person at the right time by your side to help you. So have a plan, but be open to changes in that plan. And never take your eyes off the goal.

Third, you've got to take action every day. EVERY day. So many people get the first two right, but they fail to follow through. Their first downfall may come as soon as they've set the goal and made the plan, because now they feel they've achieved something and can take a rest. Not true. Having a goal and creating a plan are the steps you take PRIOR to achievement – they are not achievements themselves.

So the moment you create your plan, take an action step. And then each day there after, do not go to bed until you have taken another step. Even if it's late and you're tired, do SOMETHING to get yourself closer to your goal.

Fourth, you've got to let go of the outcome. This sounds contrary, doesn't it? Certainly it's the most difficult step of the four to understand. But if you are desperate to achieve your goal, you will actually self-sabotage and push that goal further away from you, rather than drawing it closer.

Determination is one thing, desperation is another. Determination allows you to take calm, continuous action. But if you are desperate, you are moving out of focused action and into emotional reaction.

How do you know if you are desperate? If you have thoughts such as, "I can't be happy without this," or "I can't be successful if I don't achieve this," then you are desperate. You are telling yourself that you cannot be happy or successful in the present because you have not achieved those things.

The remedy? Letting go of the outcome and instead focusing on being excited and enthusiastic about not just the goal, but also the process itself. When you feel motivated and invigorated, you can easily visualize your goal coming to pass. This stimulates positive brain chemistry that focuses your conscious creation of your goal. Not to mention it just plain feels good and gives you all the energy you need to work on achieving your goal every single day.

You might benefit from these tips on how to take action while you're letting go of your attachment:

a) **Get rid of the negative thinking.** When you catch yourself thinking negative thoughts, find something positive to replace them with.

b) **Stop negative emotions.** When you catch yourself feeling down, find something to feel positive about. In addition, move your body. This might be jumping up and down, doing stretches or walking. Physical activity helps to banish negative emotions and makes you feel empowered.

c) **Take pleasure in the process.** Rather than viewing the journey to your goal as a burden, think of it as a pleasure in its own right.

d) **Be the best 'you' possible.** In all that you do, be honest and never let go of your integrity or do anything that would tarnish your good name. Success achieved at the expense of your honor is a hollow success at best.

e) **Banish doubt and self-criticism.** You can't be happy or successful if you don't believe in yourself and your abilities. The best way to boost self-confidence? By taking action everyday towards achieving your goal, and taking note of all the small victories and accomplishments along the way.

f) **Affirm yourself several times a day.** Acknowledge your talents, your skills, your strengths and capabilities. Know that you deserve success.

g) **Be the person you want to be – NOW.** How will you feel when your dreams come true? Start feeling that way today. What kind of person will you be when you achieve your goals? Be that person right now.

There you have it – success in four easy steps. And no matter what you want to accomplish, this mini road map can take you there.

Learn it, live it and love it, and it will be yours forever. Imagine that – the key to achieving anything you want, right here before you.

One last thing – some of you are saying to yourselves, "But I've heard this before." I wouldn't be surprised if you have. But the issue isn't whether or not you've heard it – the issue is whether or not you are LIVING it.

So tell me – are you? If not, I'd like to suggest the following...

Make a commitment to yourself right here and now that you will memorize these four steps and immediately put them into action. Commit to yourself that you will spend every day for the next 30 days using these steps to achieve a goal that you really want.

And then report back to me with the results. As you can imagine, you'll be pleasantly surprised by what you achieve.

21 Great Ways To Find Blog Topics
When you first start writing a blog the ideas come from everywhere and they seem endless. After all, you're (hopefully) writing about something you know and love, something that is dear to your heart.

But what happens after that initial burst of writing frenzy, when the ideas dry up and you're faced with a blank screen?

Here are 21 ways to find new ideas that inspire you to keep writing. And no matter what methods you choose, you'll always want to keep a log of your ideas so you don't lose them before you can write them. Remember: The idea you think of right now that is so outstanding you can't possibly forget it - is the idea you inevitably forget.

1. **Google Alerts.** If you choose only one of these 21 methods, then without a doubt this is the one to pick. Whatever your niche is, pick your best keywords, go to Google Alerts, and ask it to send you the best stories every day. Then use these as inspiration and research in writing your own blog entries.

2. **Read your competitors.** You never want to copy them, but you will find plenty of ideas of your won simply by reading their blogs.

3. **React to someone else's post.** Did you read a post that you have a strong opinion about? Do you perhaps disagree? Vehemently? Write your own post giving your own point of view. You'll find the words pouring out almost without effort, and because of your passion your readers will post more replies and send you more social media love as well.

4. **Ask yourself what's missing.** When you're reading other people's stuff, ask what they left out, what they missed, or what is going to come next. Both finding the less obvious or predicting the future can make for great posts.

5. **Read totally unrelated material,** and then ask yourself how it relates to your own niche. This can provide out-of-the-box thinking that totally rocks and again provides you with social media love.

6. **Find the pain.** Your readers have problems – what are they and how can you help?

7. **Do interviews.** Get in touch with others in your niche and ask to do a written question and answer interview. You email the questions, they write back the answers, and you've got a blog post. How easy was that? If they have a product, let them plug it – if they have an affiliate program, sign on as an affiliate and earn a commission from your post. Talk about easy content and easy money. Even if you make just a couple

of sales, you've now monetized that post.

8. **Talk about how your view has changed.** If you've been writing for your blog for a good while, go back and read some of your original posts. Do you still agree with what you wrote, or has your perspective changed? If you think differently now, write a new post referencing how you felt then versus why your views are different now.

9. **Did you make mistakes in your niche?** Talk about them. Your readers want to hear that you're human, and they want to know how you overcame your problems or lived down your naivete or foolishness.

10. **Write something funny.** Who doesn't love funny writing? If you've got a unique viewpoint on the humorous side of your niche, by all means write it down. It may be one of your post popular posts ever.

11. **Debate.** Do you have strong opinions? If so, can you find someone with equally strong opinions who disagrees with you? Posts written by two people presenting opposite viewpoints can be fascinating, and they tend to get a huge response from their readers.

12. **Make a prediction.** Go ahead, lay it on the line and predict something that's going to happen in your niche. People love to know what to expect, and if it turns out you're right, be sure to remind them of your original post by writing about it and linking to it.

13. **Sit for ideas.** Find a quiet spot, get comfortable, clear your

mind and ask yourself, "What should I write about?" Just relax, and the answers will come. Keep pen and paper handy, you're going to want to write this down.

14. **Exercise.** Go for a walk, jump up and down on a trampoline, whatever. Just get some exercise, get the blood flowing, and let the ideas come.

15. **Hold a contest.** Why not? Ask the best open ended question you can think of in your niche, and invite readers to respond. You choose the winner, and provide the prize. Or you can let your readers vote for their favorite.

16. **Write a story.** Make it an outlandish fairy tale or a modern day drama. Just relate it to your niche and use it to teach a concept. Who doesn't love stories?

17. **Look to your blog comments.** Read the comments you get and find questions you haven't answered or ideas you haven't thought of, and then write your post based on those.

18. **Do a product review.** A real one. Not one of these reviews that sells the product, but rather a review that tells the truth. Mind you, this is a two-edged sword. The more honest you are, the more your readers will love you and the more your fellow product creators may hate you if you didn't like their product.

19. **Do a book review.** Get the latest books in your niche from Amazon or Barnes and Noble, and review the books.

20. **Be ridiculous and see if anybody notices.** Write a completely tongue-in-cheek piece about something in your

niche, citing outlandish facts and using bogus experts – then see what happens. Some readers will catch on, others won't, and you'll get some great reader comments. Then make a second post letting them know it was a farce.

21. **Use guest bloggers.** Perhaps the easiest solution of all is to allow others to do your blogging for you.

The Two Obstacles to Success

We began this month's newsletter with the 4 Steps to Success, so I think it's only fair that I also tell you about the 2 Obstacles to Success. Forewarned is forearmed, and by knowing in advance what can stop you from realizing your goals, you'll be able to do what's necessary to overcome these obstacles and move straight through to victory.

The first obstacle is engaging in limiting beliefs. Need I say more? Well, maybe...

If we get what we think about, and we think we don't have what it takes to accomplish something, what happens? We don't accomplish it. If we believe that we don't deserve success, do we get it? Not likely. And if we're always being negative, thinking negative, speaking negative, what happens? Nothing good.

We achieve what we believe. Period. Not what we hope for, desire, wish for, etc. There used to be a computer expression – garbage in, garbage out. And it's the same way with your beliefs – bad thoughts in, bad results out.

Whatever it takes, whatever you've got to do, find a way to lose the limiting beliefs and replace them with positive, boundless limitless thoughts of success.

The second obstacle to success? Is giving up too soon.

There is a quote I like:

"While one person hesitates because he feels inferior, the other is busy making mistakes and becoming superior." -Henry C. Link

You've no doubt heard the story of the man who mined for gold and gave up just inches shy of hitting the mother lode. It's the same way in anything – every time you give up, you lose. Wayne Gretsky said, "You miss 100% of the shots you don't take." You've got to keep shooting, keep moving towards your goal, because it is only through quitting that you can fail.

If you do not quit, you cannot fail because you are not done yet.

As Winston Churchill said, "Never, never, never, never give up."

You've Been Hacked!

Hackers LOVE to attack Wordpress sites, making your life miserable and potentially losing you revenue and time, not to mention content and piece of mind. And despite all the warnings out there, we still hear of someone almost daily who's been hacked. Hopefully for you it's not too late to take some simple but effective precautions. With that in mind, here are some simple tips to keep your Wordpress sites safe:

1. Stop thinking it can't happen to you. IT CAN. You might have the cutest little site on kittens – who would want to hack that? Guaranteed, for whatever demented reason, someone somewhere does.

2. Treat your username like a password. Never, ever use the default "admin." And don't use something easy like your email address, either. Create a tough username that no one could possibly guess. Best bet? Use uppercase, lowercase, numbers and symbols, just like a password.

3. Use a super strong password. Again, use upper and lowercase letters, numbers and symbols. Make it long and totally random.

4. Write your passwords down on paper, or use a password software.

5. Never use the same username or the same password for different sites. This way if one of your sites does get hacked, the others won't fall like dominoes, too.

6. Change your passwords often, especially if you give anyone temporary access into your account or if an employee or outsourcer leaves.

7. Backup often, REALLY often. Use a Wordpress plugin to do this automatically for you. Keep your last 3-4 backups in a separate location.

8. Sure, all of this seems like a pain, but compare it to being hacked and you'll realize it's well worth the extra hassle.

Why Hate Mail is GOOD – And What To Do About It

If you're an online marketer, you're probably going to get flamed now and then.

But you know what? Getting hate mail is actually a GOOD thing.

In a nutshell, here's why...

If you're trying to please everyone, you're pleasing no one. If you're pleasing no one, well, you're probably not making any money.

The reason we choose a niche is because we're targeting a certain market. Everyone else need not apply. It's like in sales – you've got to get through some "no's" to get to the "yes's."

But online is slightly different because instead of people simply telling you "no," you'll have a few who go off the deep end and write you a nasty email.

What should you do?

First, be happy. If you're pissing somebody off that bad, you're also making others happy. Do you think Rush Limbaugh (a famous ultra-conservative radio talk show host) pisses a lot of people off? You bet! Yet he's a multi-multi-millionaire.

Second, don't reply. People who send you hate mail are trolls, and the moment you enter into a conversation with a troll you have lost. So just ignore it.

Third, you might talk about the email to your readers. Why would you do something so seemingly crazy? People like to "belong." And when they read the email, they will see it as written by someone outside of your clique. It becomes an "us" vs "them" sort of thing, with you and your readers being the "us." Your audience will appreciate that they are a part of YOUR group and will see the offending party as an outsider, thereby strengthening your bond with your people. It can even make your sales go up for that day.

So next time you get hate mail, smile and know that you are indeed doing something right.

One more thing – be sure to delete and blacklist the sender from every email list you've got. The best thing about this kind of person is never hearing from them again.

What Managers Can Learn From Programmers
One trait that a lot of programmers have in common is laziness. Of course there's something of an unflattering stereotype of programmers which tends to involve a gut and disheveled facial hair. But that's not what we're talking about here. Rather, programmers are lazy because they are constantly taking shortcuts.

In fact, did you know that the term 'hack' was originally used in a coding sense to refer to 'inelegant' coding solutions that got the job done? This in turn was what ultimately led to the 'lifehack' trend that is now sweeping the globe and it's why so many of us are constantly looking for shortcuts and more efficient ways of doing things. But what does all this have to do with managers and business owners?

Time to Hack Your Business

When a programmer finds themselves doing *anything* more than once, they will almost always end up writing a program to do it instead. Making long lists over and over again? Why not make a piece of code that will do it for you instead? You'll invest more time up-front but ultimately you'll never have to do that job again and you'll save countless hours.

Using the same routine in a piece of code over and over again? A programmer will write a 'sub routine' which they can 'call' at any time to perform that function on an automated basis. Even the *structure* of programming is built this way.

But it's not really laziness, rather it is 'efficiency' and it's 'systems thinking'. Why *would* you spend lots of time doing the same thing over and over again when a program could do it for you? And especially when time equals money?

So how do you approach your business with this mindset? The solution is to start thinking about your business more like a system and to think about the smaller component aspects of your business as 'microsystems' that make up the whole.

Now you can treat it like code. Look at the jobs you are repeating most often. How could they be done better and more quickly to save you time and money? Likewise, how could you save yourself from making mistakes?

Sometimes, this will actually *mean* asking a coder to write you a piece of software to do what you previously had your team doing. In other cases, it will simply mean changing the order that work is done or introducing a new flow chart or checklist. Either way, everything can be made more efficient and thus save you time *and* money.

5 Keys to a Money Making Online Business

We're always trying to over complicate things, aren't we? Making things appear more difficult than they really are. Why is that?

The other day I saw a break down of the 7 things you need to build your online marketing business, which was 2 more than you really need. Here's my list: Network, List Build, Focus, Take Action, Produce. That's right, just 5 things.

So let's break each one down to it's simplest form:

1. Network. Make friends with other marketers in your niche, whatever that niche might be. When you need help (such as promotion) call on them. Help them out when they need it.

Why is networking so important? 3 reasons: First, working from home can be lonely, daunting, and just plain difficult. It's easy to procrastinate. It's easy to get bogged down on some little obstacle. But when you've got others to turn to for morale support, it gets a whole lot easier.

Second, you can get quick help. Having trouble loading that widget or formatting that ebook? Contact your friend who's a wiz at it and you've got the help you need. Be there to help them, too.

Third, promotion. Do you think it's just coincidence when you get 5 or 10 emails promoting the same product? No. Those are friends of the person launching the product. It can make all the difference in the world to have a list of people to turn to when it comes to promoting your products. Without networking, your list is going to be a whole lot smaller.

2. Build a list. No need to spell this one out – if you've got a list then you've got people to promote to. The better and bigger the list, the more prosperous your business can be. If you're not list building, begin now - as in TODAY.

3. Focus. I know I've hit on this before, but here goes – STAY FOCUSED! I wanted to add a swear word after that for emphasis, but in the interest of keeping this PG I won't. So many times I see people jump from this to that to the thing over there and around and around

and they never stay focused on one thing for more than a day or two and then they wonder why they're aren't successful.

Pick something. ONE thing. Then FOCUS on that one thing until you've got it done. Eliminate distractions. If need be, REMOVE distractions from your immediate vicinity. Set a work schedule and STICK to the work schedule.

Here's something to make it simple:

The more focused you are, the more money you will earn. Period.

4. Take Action. Don't just plan and daydream, DO. Move forward every single day by taking a real action that gets you closer to your goals.

5. Produce products. LOTS of products. There are those who buy lots of products and those who PRODUCE lots of products. Who do you think is more successful?

Let's put it another way – what are your odds of success if you produce one product versus 10 products? 100 products? Not all of your products will be grand slams, but when you produce enough of them then some of them will be hits. Also, by producing your own products you're also building your own reputation online, which furthers your success. So take the plunge and begin producing products to sell in your business – in fact, make a HABIT out of product production.

That's it. Do these 5 things day in and day out starting today and continuing as long as you're an online marketer, and success will almost undoubtedly be yours.

You Don't Have To Be Super Smart To Succeed Online
The kid who got straight A's in school is probably the most successful person from that class, right? Actually, no. While good grades and a high I.Q. can be helpful, they not only don't guarantee success - they sometimes hamper success.

After all, life is not school. And the skills it takes to get great grades don't always transfer over into running a successful online business. Heck, I know people who struggled in high school and never made to college who are pulling down 6 and 7 figure incomes online. How do they do it? By possessing the following traits...

1. They have the drive to succeed. How you define success will determine exactly what this means to you. Success for you might be making as much money as possible, it might be furthering a cause of yours, or it might be one of a hundred other things. Whatever it is, you've got to have a need to reach this success that you can feel in your bones. It should be your total focus so that your mind is constantly at work finding ways to make it happen.

2. They're good at networking. Even online, or perhaps especially online, it's important that you build relationships with your fellow marketers and your customers. And even if

you're not a born schmoozer, don't worry – networking is a skill like any other that can be learned. Work on building yourself a large network of people you can turn to for advice, assistance and so forth, and always focus on what you can do for them.

3. They stay focused. Imagine you're driving your car and you decide to go 5 different directions – at once. How far will you get? Or imagine chasing 5 different rabbits all at the same time – how many will you catch? Business is no different. Decide what you're going to do and then do it, rather than falling for the flavor-of-the-week business idea.

4. They're persistent. You're not going to build a super-profitable business overnight. And if you're looking at others thinking they became successful in a flash, know that in reality their success probably took years. Remember, nothing worth having comes easy, and persistence does conquer all.

5. They stand on their own two feet. I've seen people purchase a course on how to do something online, such as build a website or get more traffic. Then they bombard the author with a hundred different questions rather than figure anything out for themselves. Are they ever successful? I doubt it. Being an online marketer, or any type of entrepreneur, carries with it a certain autonomy. So don't expect others to hold your hand.

6. They work first, they work hard and they play later. Sometimes MUCH later. You know those stories of working

2 hours a day and then laying on the beach? That's for AFTER you make it big and you can hire somebody to oversee things for you. Maybe. Or even when you do make it big in online marketing, you may find that you still work hard. But either way, in the beginning you'll be working long hours to get your business up and running. And yes, work does come before play if you want to be successful. If you want to play first, you might as well ditch the idea of being an online marketer and stick with a job.

7. Learn to outsource. There is only so much you can accomplish by yourself, even when you are working long hours. So yes, you've got to outsource. The first thing to outsource is anything you're not good at, whether that's website building, product creation, or whatever. Because if you're not good as something, it makes more sense to bring in an expert than to spend weeks trying to master it yourself. Then as you begin earning more and more, you can also outsource more and more.

To be an online marketer, you don't need to be the next Einstein. Your grades in school don't matter a hill of beans. What DOES matter is what you do here and now. Adopt the above 7 traits and you are already halfway to growing an online business that can take care of you for the rest of your life.

11 Steps to Quitting Your Job and Pursuing Your Online Business

Are you still working at a job you don't particularly like? Maybe its time to set the goal to get the life you seek by building your online business and telling your boss you'll be leaving for something better – working at home in your pj's! Okay not so dramatic. But you get the point.

1. Focus your online business on your passion. There's no sense building an online information type of business - no matter how potentially lucrative – around a topic that doesn't interest you. If you do, you'll end up right where you are now – chained to a "job" that's no fun for you. Instead, find a way to monetize whatever it is that you love online. And 9 times out of 10, it's offering information on that topic, whether you sell the information or give it away and make your money on advertising and affiliate products.

2. Get your spouse on board. Starting your own business is challenging enough without having to hear from your spouse that you are wasting time and money. So get them on your side by talking to them and asking them for their support and encouragement.

3. Get an accountability partner. This might be your spouse, or more likely it will be a fellow online marketer. Tell each other what your goals are – both long range and on a daily basis – and then check in with each other daily to see if you've met your goals. Just knowing you'll have to answer to

someone can be a great motivator.

4. Don't worry about what others think. What – your neighbor thinks you're nuts? Your best friend just shakes his head when you talk about your online marketing business? So what? It's your life and it's your choice. If they're really your friends, they'll support you. If they don't, then you shouldn't give it (or perhaps them) another thought.

5. Build your network. Find the movers and shakers in your niche and find ways to promote them and network with them. This way when you launch a new product or even simply make a new blogpost, you've got people who can help you spread the word.

6. Get your finances in order. It can be challenging enough to start an online business. Adding the pressure of having no money in reserves can be downright daunting and even paralyzing. That's why you want to pay off your bills as best you can and also set some money aside for a rainy day. And when you have your first big online success (and you will) spend a little of it and save a lot of it.

7. Plan your work and then work your plan. Building a business by hit and miss is hard – following a step-by-step plan is easy. With your end goal in mind, make a chronological list of all the things you need to do to reach that goal. Then start at #1 and get to work. When you find other things you need to do, add them into the list. And when you find you don't need some of things you did, cross them off. You plan should

be fluid enough to accommodate new information and change, and concrete enough to let you know what you'll be doing and when you'll be doing it.

8. Write down your goals for the day first thing every morning, and then don't go to bed until you achieve those goals. Make the goals large enough to keep you interested and small enough that you can accomplish them. This step alone can triple your productivity and keep you inspired to continually move towards your goal.

9. Forget the perks. Maybe your job offers benefits or bonuses that you won't have in your online business. Does this mean you should give up your dream and stay in the job you don't like? I can't answer that for you, but think on this: If you're earning six figures in your own business, can't you purchase your own insurance and give yourself all the bonuses you like? Not to mention the fact that you set your own schedule, which can accommodate far more vacation time than any job will ever offer you.

10. Make motivation a natural part of your day. It's easy in the beginning to get excited about your business, but as with anything else, it can become routine after awhile. So start your day off with something that motivates you; it might be envisioning your next success, meditating on what you will achieve this day, reading motivational materials, etc. And make this a habit you never break from. It's far easier to stay motivated than it is to re-motivate yourself after you've lost

some of your enthusiasm.

11. Set a deadline for leaving your job. If you count down each day until the day you plan on quitting your job, the entire process will seem much more real to you, and you'll find that you make the best use of the time you have available.

And remember, you don't have to get it perfect – you just have to get it going.

9 Easy Steps To Failure

Let's face it – success is over rated. Sure, everyone wants to have great relationships, profitable businesses, lots of money in the bank and luxurious vacations to exotic locations. But it takes a real hero to successfully fail. It takes guts, it takes planning, it takes hard work... errr... wait a minute...

It doesn't take any of those things to fail, now does it?

So what does it take to wake up in the middle of the night in a cold sweat, realizing that you're throwing your life away in useless activities that go nowhere and accomplish nothing? How do you ensure you'll never have that dream home or that million dollar retirement? Don't worry - failure is surprisingly easy when you know how.

That's why I've assembled 9 of the very best methods to completely and totally ward off success and ensure you enjoy imminent and complete failure.

Below are 9 easy steps to failure:

1) **Do NOT define what success means to you.** This is the grand daddy of all failure techniques; one that works nearly every single time. It's only when you clearly define your goal that you can reach it. That's why you want to choose entirely ambiguous goals, such as: "I want to lose weight" or "I want to make more money." If you're foolish enough to make your goal specific, such as: "I want to lose 28 pounds, run the mile in 9 minutes and get my cholesterol down to 150 by September 30th" then you've just quadrupled your chance of succeeding. It's only by setting specific, measurable goals that you can achieve those goals. By refusing to pinpoint exactly what you want to achieve before you start, you'll fail almost before you begin.

2) **Do NOT make a plan.** The moment you make specific plans for how to achieve your goals, you're on your way to success. That's why you want to simply trust that it will all somehow happen, without you doing any planning whatsoever. Remember, those poor slobs who make specific goals and then formulate plans on how to achieve those goals are the ones who get stuck with success.

3) **Do procrastinate every chance you get.** There is nothing you can do today that can't be put off until tomorrow. Successful people make specific goals, formulate plans to reach their goals, and then they work their plans. No wonder

160

why they end up enduring success after success. To be the best failure you can be, do nothing today that gets you any closer to reaching your goals. Put everything off until tomorrow, because as you and I both know, tomorrow never comes. Perfecting procrastination is one of the biggest insurance policies you can have against success.

4) **If you have to do something, focus on the things you're bad at.** Successful marketers focus on their strengths and outsource their weaknesses. For example, one online heavy hitter I know is amazing at SEO, but he's terrible at content creation. Thus he outsources all of his writing while focusing his efforts on ranking his websites at #1. This method has earned him hundreds of thousands of dollars in just the past 36 months. If he was smart about failing, he would focus all his efforts on writing, and leave the SEO for when he finally gets good at content creation.

5) **Be consumptive and not productive.** Being consumptive is being passive: Watching TV, checking email, chatting online, etc. Being productive is being active: Creating content, contacting clients, building your next website, etc. Here's a not so startling fact: Your personal ratio between consumptive and productive accurately identifies how happy and successful you are. That's why if you want to fail, you want to be as consumptive as possible. And as an added bonus, you'll also be far less happy as well. And you know as well as I do that happy people are just annoying, anyway,

right?

6) **Surround yourself with people who don't support you.**
You'll find there are 3 different kinds of people in life: The
Encouragers, The Don't Care's, and the The Schadenfreudes.
The Encouragers will actively encourage you every step of
the way to success, and they're invaluable to anyone silly
enough to want to succeed. But all you need to do is avoid
these folks and try to go it alone, because almost no one can
stay energized and motivated when they're totally isolated.
The Don't Care's act like you're speaking another language
when you try to tell them what you're trying to accomplish,
so they're good at discouraging you from success. And the
Shadenfreudes actually revel and take great satisfaction in
your failures, so be sure to keep a few of these around you at
all times.

7) **Don't join groups of like-minded people.** No mastermind
groups – those things make people succeed like crazy. No
Meetup.com to find like-minded people, no Yahoo! Or
Google Groups, no Facebook for finding your topic. Those
things are strictly off limits, since you can wind up building
an entire support team who cheer you on to success.

8) **Do NOT get a coach.** Personal trainers, business and life
coaches, etc. are all conspiring to make you succeed. Avoid
them at all costs. Heck, I've personally coached students who
saw phenomenal success in short periods of time, so buyer

beware – hiring a coach can cost you your failure.

9) **Close your mind.** Thinking unconventionally and taking the less obvious route can bring about goal achievement and success in record time. For example, a friend of mine wanted to make his living as a motivational speaker. Everyone knows that to make your living speaking you have to begin with free speeches for a few years. Then you work your way up the ladder, moving into low paying gigs and ever so gradually increasing your fee until after a decade or so you can get the high paying jobs. He skipped all of that and simply decided to start with the high paying gigs, and within months he was earning a very nice six figure income. If only he had closed his mind and taken the conventional route, he'd still be struggling today.

There you have it – 9 essential skills to ensuring your total and complete failure.

And if you choose to be an anarchist and make some kind of radical success out of our life, your business, your goals and your dreams, then I'm afraid I've just inadvertently provided you with the secrets to success. Of course you'll have to decode them from the skills above, but I suspect you are very much up to the task.

Creating Great Content for BORING Niches

Not long ago the "Boring Web Content Challenge" was held. Now – how would you like to be a finalist (or worse yet, the WINNER) in that contest? *"Hey everybody, come to my site because I have the most boring content on the entire web!"* No thanks.

It's a mantra you've heard time and time again – write great, interesting, exciting, sharable content. But what if you're in a boring niche? Or working for a boring client in a boring niche? How do you get readers excited about mundane topics like locksmiths or plumbing, or even icky topics like personal injury lawyers or rash creams?

Here are 10 tips to help you create interesting content ideas for even the most boring of niches.

1. First, change your perspective before you write anything. If you think it's boring, your readers will, too. Everything is interesting if presented in an interesting manner. It's simply a matter of finding the right angles to present your content. And the first step is to get fascinated in your topic so your enthusiasm will show in your writing.

2. Find the golden number nuggets. Dig out the industry statistics and find the fascinating bits that pull people into your story. Do you sell nails? How many nails go into building the typical house? Is your niche floor coverings? If you took all the carpet made in one month, how big of a city/state would it cover? Numbers fascinate when used in a way people can easily grasp and share with others.

3. Use stories and anecdotes. Let's say you sell instructions on

how to refinish furniture. "14 year old Annie was always the shy type, afraid to speak up and withdrawn, lacking confidence to do even the simplest of things. Then she got our beginner's instructions for refinishing simple antique chairs. Within a month she'd finished her first project, and now a year later she's refinished over a dozen pieces, resold 9 of them for substantial profit that she's put away for college, and kept or given away the rest of the pieces. Most important of all, she's gained a new sense of accomplishment and confidence which has spilled over into other areas of her life." Wow, that's pretty exciting!

4. Do a daily question and answer. Each day create an "ask an expert" blogpost or video in which you answer one question. Create interaction, likes and shares by getting real people to ask questions through social media such as Facebook.

5. Talk about what's wrong in your niche. Maybe legislation is pending that could hurt your industry, or someone in your niche is ripping people off. Be the leader and speak up about it. You'll not only capture the attention of your readers – you'll likely get links from other sites as people join the conversation.

6. Promote a cause. Sometimes when you run out of things to say about your business and your niche, it's time to look outside of your business and find a cause to make your own. For example, a personal injury lawyer who's helping homeless puppies and kittens to find new homes – that's not

only unexpected, it's even warm and fuzzy – literally. And if your business is strictly virtual, you can still choose a cause and make it your own. Put real faces on it – furry or human – and tell why you and your business strongly support this cause. If you can choose a cause aligned with your business, so much the better. For example, a food niche might choose a program to feed the hungry, while a remodeling/building/decorating business might choose something like Habitat for Humanity.

7. Hold content contests. Get your readers to create content for you, based around the keywords you choose. The better the prize, the more entries you're likely to get. Pick the top entries and then get them to get their friends to vote for the best one with retweets and Facebook shares. Publicize the contest to get more entries, more press and more backlinks.

8. Become a hub for industry content. Who says you need to write all of your website's content yourself? Ask other industry leaders to contribute if they like.

9. Use images. We've said it before and we'll say it again – people stay on your blog or website longer when you use interesting, compelling and relevant images.

10. Stretch. Okay, so your niche is car accessories – why not do an article on the top coolest cars in movies? Or maybe your niche is math tutoring – again, find the movies that use math and talk about those. It's a great way to get your audience to relate to your products.

Even the most mundane of topics can become interesting – you've just got to find the right angle to write about.

What Are You Creating – Income? Or Wealth? And Why Should You Care?

Here's an interesting notion from Dan Kennedy in his own words: "One of the lessons I learned slowly and painfully has to do with income versus wealth." So what's the difference? According to Dan, sales and profits are important, and they're what most entrepreneurs focus on. But they're not wealth and they don't produce wealth. Wealth, he says, comes from creating valuable assets. You can either work all your life to create income, or you can focus on building assets and come to a place where you have so much wealth, the income takes care of itself.

For example, opening your own little cafe creates income. But creating a duplicateable system – like McDonald's – creates wealth. Now, let's take Dan's income versus wealth theory into the realm of internet marketing and see what happens: Let's say you create an info product and sell it – that would be income. You can make a lot of money doing this, but it's always work. You're having to continuously plug along to make it happen. And it's different every time. You've got no real system, it's more of a seat of your pants kind of thing each time you create and launch a new product.

But if you were to develop a system for creating and selling profitable info products, that's wealth. With your system, you can now plug writers into the process, tell them what to do, and then

167

hand it over to your copywriter, webmaster and affiliate manager to make the profits. With this system in place, you can launch a new product every month, every week or even every day if you scale it up.

Imagine that – being in 15 different niches, launching a product in each niche twice a month – could you create wealth that way? And if you can systematize your process for picking product topics, you might even go to some island somewhere while you team does it for you. It sort of boggles the mind, doesn't it? Here's a challenge for you for the next month: See how many of your activities you can systematize. For example, checking your stats: If you do it whenever you think of it, it's not a system. If you do it at 9 a.m. Each Monday morning so you can compare it to the previous periods, you've now got a system.

The more systems you have in place, the easier your work will become. When you're ready, you'll be able to hand off work to a virtual assistant simply by showing him or her exactly how each system works and what to do. It's no different than training a new employee at McDonald's how to make a Big Mac. There is a system – the system works – and now you can outsource that work to someone else.

And when you decide to sell off some or all of your business assets, they will be worth far more because anyone, ANYONE, will be able to plug themselves into your systems and do exactly what you do with the same level of success. This will quadruple the value of your business. Sort of like selling McDonald's franchises.

Work Smarter, Not Stupider

Look, you're either working smart or you're wasting time. And since time is literally the most precious commodity anyone owns, wasting it isn't the most prudent thing to do, is it? I mean, if I were to ask you, "Hey, do you want to waste 500 days on Facebook," would you ever say yes? Yet people have done exactly that. And when I say 500 days, I mean 500 24 hour days.

Ouch.

That's why it's so important to become an expert at managing your time, so you can spend more of it having the life you want instead of building the life you hope to have some day. In other words, work smart and you will realize your goals far faster.

You'll notice the original article on 21 Time Management Tips is very polite and laid back, while my own version (below) of the list is a bit more opinionated. But hey, I'm not here to make you feel good, I'm here to see if I can blast you into major productivity and hyper success.

(Source of the original 21 Time Mangement Tips: http://bit.ly/21tmtips)

1. Do the important stuff first. That's first, before anything else. As in, FIRST. Yes, it's basic. It's also amazing how many

people check their email and their social media and read the newspaper and check YouTube and so forth before doing the important stuff (which as a consequence usually doesn't get done.)

2. Say "no." A lot. Know when to say "no."

3. Sleep until you're done sleeping. For most people this is 7.5 hours. Scrimping on sleep means you won't be as productive the next day.

4. Focus. FOCUS. Imagine you're hypnotized and can only focus on the task at hand. Nothing else exists, including your email.

5. Start early. Start work early in the morning and start on projects long before they're due. Procrastination will kill your ambitions, your dreams and your goals. Therefore procrastination is your sworn enemy. Treat it as such.

6. Details? We don't need no stinking details. Get it done and get it out the door. If you're shooting for perfection, you're aiming for failure.

7. Turn your most important tasks into HABITS. If they're as important as brushing your teeth and combing your hair, then make them as much of a priority.

8. Blow up the TV, smash the game console and stop fooling around on the Internet. No, you don't need to watch that cute kitten compilation video. Now get back to work.

9. Set time limits and deadlines. Live by them. Die by them. Work expands to fill the time allotted, so only allot what you

need and no more.

10. Take a walk. When you finish one task, take a short walk before you start the next. It'll clear your head.

11. Don't worry about your 46 item to-do list. Focus on one thing at a time and only one thing. Breathe.

12. Exercise and eat like a sane person. You're given ONE body and one body only. Treat it like it's one of your most precious possessions, because until they perfect the body transplant, it's your one and only home.

13. Do less. This is like saying "no" only you maybe already said "yes" and now you realize that was a mistake. Don't compound the mistake by following through (unless you made a promise to someone else.) You were going to write that article, now you realize it's a lousy topic so don't write the thing. You get the idea.

14. Make Monday better by doing some work on the weekend. Two days of no work makes it darn difficult to get started on Monday. So spend 2-4 hours working on Saturday and Sunday, too. This gives you plenty of time off, and primes you for a roaring start on Monday. Plus, if you really catch up on work, you can now take one weekday afternoon off.

15. Organize your stuff. Spending 30 minutes trying to find an article isn't productive. So get organized, and this is key – STAY organized. Every day before you stop work, put everything where it belongs so you can find it again when you need it.

16. There is no 'down time.' You're waiting in line? Driving your car? On the elliptical at the gym? Then listen to podcasts that can help you in your business, or do something that's productive. If nothing else, knit in the doctor's waiting room – it's a great stress reliever. Seriously.

17. Lock yourself in. Or more specifically, lock everyone else out. Don't come out until you finish your current task. Radical but it works.

18. Don't flake on your plan. Once you decide to do something, DO IT.

19. Batch it, baby. To a point. If you need to make 5 phone calls, answer 12 emails and write two blogposts, then do those things in batches. Once you make one phone call you're in the right mindset to quickly make the others. Once you answer one email, the other 11 are are a snap. But, if you need to do several similar things that each take a long time, batching can be a bad idea because of burn out. In that case, do one, take a break while you do something small, and then go back and start on the second one. Doing a small task between large tasks resets your head and gives you a better sense of accomplishment.

20. Find time for stillness and silliness. It's important to practice stillness for a few minutes each day to reduce anxiety and clear your head. Focus on your breathing and on relaxing each part of your body. Silliness is important, too. Read something funny. Make silly faces in the mirror or at your

child. Jump rope or hula hoop. In other words, play with your inner child each day, if only for a few moments.

21. Eliminate the excess and non-essential. Simplify. Figure out what's important and what deserves your time, and then ditch the rest.

One last thing – Love your life. Love your day. Love your friends and family, and Love your work. Most of all – Love yourself.

Headline Idea Cheat Sheet

You might want to save this and keep it next to your computer. Then next time you're stuck for a headline, just refer back to it to get your creative juices flowing. And don't save this just for sales letters – you can use this for any headline – ezine subject lines, blog post headlines, article headlines, etc.

HINT: You can also use this list when you're stuck for ideas of what to write about!

1) **Tie Into Breaking News** – anytime you can tie your writing into current events you'll grab more eyeballs.

2) **Call Out Your Reader** – is your reader somehow missing the boat? Call them on it in the headline.

3) **Offer a Proposition** – if you give me 5 minutes, I'll show you how to erase 10 years from your face.

4) **Be Shocking** – this one is a little risky but the benefit can be tremendous. Note: Be sure you're not using shock value simply for the sake of shock – it's also got to tie directly into

your message.

5) **Use Sex** – yes, sex captures attention, and if you can tie it into your message, so much the better. Just make sure it's not x-rated.

6) **Be an Advocate** – your reader has enemies, so take the position of advocate for your reader. For example, if you're offering natural remedies, the enemy might be profit seeking drug companies pushing deadly pills to make a fast buck.

7) **Curiosity** – the more curious the better. People have an insatiable need to KNOW, so if you can make them curious enough in the headline, they won't be able to leave until they find the answer in your copy.

8) **Odd Cause and Effect** – can you erase acne with a frying pan? Or maybe show someone how to increase their income by spending MORE? Then you might have a great headline.

9) **Let's Make a Deal!** - are you making a dynamite offer that gives tremendous value for a relatively low price? Or offering tremendous benefits just for reading your blog post? Then state it right there in the headline.

10) **Offer Revenge** – who doesn't want to get even with the person or business who did them wrong? Promise them in your headline that they can, and they'll read your copy to the end.

11) **Tell a Story** – no, you won't tell the whole story in the headline, but you can get a good start on one. What happens when someone says to you, "Once upon a time..." You're

riveted, right? It's in our programming to listen closely to stories, and they are still one of the best, yet least utilized tools in our marketing arsenals.

12) **Ask a Hot Question** - "Do you know 4 ways to make $1000 cash in the next 3 hours?" "How can you get people to obey your every wish?" You get the idea.

13) **Do the "If" or "When" Shuffle** - "If you like ___, you'll love ___." or "When you take these 3 steps, you'll get this benefit."

14) **Do the "If" and "Then" Sequence** - "If you do x, then you'll get y."

15) **Show Frustration** – "Don't you hate it when you spend an hour writing the perfect email – and no one responds?"

16) **Name Drop** – "Dustin Hoffman confided to me that..." or "John Delavera says the best membership site on the planet is..."

17) **Hit The Emotional Button** - "Stop living in fear of..." Few things grab your readers' or prospects' attention like accessing their emotions.

18) **Add or Solve a Mystery** – Is there something in your niche that hasn't been solved, and you may have the answer? Or can you create a mystery of your own?

19) **Use a Startling/Bizarre/Attention Grabbing Photo/Picture** – have you seen those ads that use weird faces? Usually the picture has nothing to do with the ad, but you look anyway. If you can find an attention grabbing photo that DOES go with

your writing, by all means place it at the top. Photos that need explanation are the best, since people will read your copy to find out what's happening in the picture.

20) **Use Urgency** – Setting a deadline in the headline eliminates the reader's desire to procrastinate reading what you've got to say. "World Ends at 5 p.m. Today!"

21) **Be Scandalous** – can you create a scandal or expose one in your niche? Then you may have the hottest headline yet.

22) **Confirm Their Fear** – if your readers already hold a fear or a suspicion, go ahead and confirm it – they'll appreciate the validation and be open to what you have to say.

23) **Debunk a Myth** – is there a common line of thought in your niche that just isn't true? Debunk it and you'll be the instant authority in your reader's eyes.

24) **Make a Bold Prediction** – go out on that limb to make a startling prediction and not only will people read your writing – they're also more likely to remember what you say.

25) **Break News** – being one of the first to report a new development makes for a great headline and excellent reading.

26) **Attack** – your reader's don't like something or someone – maybe it's as mundane as housework, or perhaps it's the government, the media, banks or the drudgery of answering emails. Whatever it is, attack it head on and then offer a solution.

27) **Offer a Cheaper, Easier, Faster or Better Solution** – your

readers have a problem and you've got a superior solution, so let them know that in the headline

28) **Use an Off-The-Wall or Compelling Quote** - "You Can't Handle The Truth!" or "I Buy When Other People Are Selling" come to mind.

Winning Headlines

Sometimes it really does pay to "cheat." After all, why would you reinvent the wheel when it's already been invented? Sure, you might improve the wheel, build something new to go on top of those wheels, or find an entirely new use for the wheel, but the basics – the wheel shape itself – stays the same.

And so it is with swipe files – especially headline swipe files. When you've got formulas that work, you only need to modify those formulas to fit your own particular need.

Eugene Schwartz' copy sold well over a billion dollars worth of products in dozens of different markets.

Now that's success you can't argue with. His clients spent millions of dollars testing Schwartz' copy with their own money, so we know what worked. After all, an advertiser does not continue to run an advertisement unless it's making him/her money.

Headlines That Paint A Picture...

a) "Pain Causing Poisons Literally Pour Out Of Your Body!"
b) "Fat Destroyer Foods"

c) "At 42, I Have To Cut 2 Inches Off My Hair Every Two Months. Otherwise, It Might Very Well Grow Right Down Past My Waist."

d) "This Woman Is Slimming Her Waistline – By Blowing Out The Candles On A Imaginary Cake!"

e) "Every Cell Of Your Face Has A Clock In It! Here's How To Wind Those Clocks Backwards!"

f) "Turns Up Your Digestive Furnace And Burns Flab Right Out F Your Body!"

g) "Pick Yourself A Fortune From The Money Trees"

Question Headlines

a) "Are The Foods You Are Eating Today Starving Your Brain?"

b) "Is This The World's Easiest Yoga?"

c) "Do You Have The Courage To Earn Half A Million Dollars A Year!"

d) "Will This Be The Most Explosive Turn Around In The History Of The Stock Market?"

e) "Is It Immoral To Make Money This Easily?"

f) "Why Haven't People In Debt Been Told These Facts?"

g) "Is It Worth $2 To You To Banish Ugly Cellulite Forever?"

h) "Want To Bowl More Strikes?"

i) "Why Haven't TV Owners Been Told These Facts?"

Rapid Results Headlines

a) "Look Years Younger, Pounds Lighter In 10 Short Days!"

b) "Change Your Life In The Next Week."

c) "How To Build A Memory In 4 Short Weeks – So Powerful It Is Beyond Your Wildest Dreams Today!"

d) "Instant Beauty! Hollywood Plastic Surgeon Releases 7-Day Crash Course Towards New Youth And Beaut.

e) "Her Eyesight Was Born Again – Returned To Normal In A Single Day."

f) "Instant Relaxation!"

g) "Let This Machine Work On Your Mind For One Evening, And I Guarantee That Your Friends Will Gasp In Astonishment At The Feats Of Mental Magic You Can Perform That Very Next Morning."

h) "One Day With This Man Could Make You Rich!"

Big Promise Headlines

a) "Feel 20 Years Younger, Live 20 Years Longer!"

b) "Want To Lose Up To 15 Pounds A Month? Then Eat 6 Times A Day – Not Three!"

"World's First Effortless Exerciser!"

c) "How To Turn Your Child Into A Classroom Wizard

d) "Is It Possible? An Automatic Income For Life Of $20,000... $50,000... $100,000 A Year Without Working... From A Business That Runs Itself!"

e) "how To Read People Like A Book!"

f) "How To Make Anybody Like You!"

g) "This Book Could Remove Your Fear Of Death Forever."

h) "From Four Packs A Day To Zero In 4 Hours!"

Conclusion

I want to leave you with something I read years ago. I can't even tell you anymore where I read it or who wrote it – all I know is that to this day I still occasionally go back and reread it just to check my own attitude and make sure I'm on the right path.

Enjoy...

The Winner – is always part of the answer;

The Loser – is always part of the problem.

The Winner – always has a plan;

The Loser – always has an excuse.

The Winner – says, "Let me do it for you."

The Loser – says, "That's not my job."

The Winner – sees an answer for every problem;

The Loser – sees a problem for every answer.

The Winner – sees a green near every sand trap;

The Loser – sees 2 or 3 sand traps near every green.

The Winner – says, "It may be difficult but it's possible."

The Loser – says, "It may be possible but it's too difficult."

Be a Winner!

PS: Thank you very much for reading this book. I very much value your time and input. Please take the time to leave a review for this book in Amazon.

Other Resources

33 Essential Resources for Developers and Designers

How-to guides, videos, lists, analysis and galleries all broken down into three lists: Inspiration, Design and Development.

http://bit.ly/33devtools

28 Ways to Make Money With Your Website

This might be the most complete list I've seen on how to monetize your websites, as well as the one with the most thorough explanations of how each of the 28 methods work.

http://bit.ly/28moneytips

Free Training.

Go to http://mulazz.com/infomaster to sign up for free for the step by step training that will teach you the fastest way to create, package and sell digital information products online. You will learn the following in this 5 day training:

- Day 1: Learn the why, when, what and how of creating original content information
- Day 2: Product creation, market selection and positioning
- Day 3: Packaging, presentation and fulfillment. A super EZ system for creating info products that people love
- Day 4: The selling process in 3 easy steps + the publisher model, Expert model and Hybrid model

- Day 5: Advanced profit strategies, the profit ladder and the big payday system

Plus you will discover:

- Where to get ideas for information products
- How to implement fast without worry or stress
- Time management – getting it done on schedule
- Outsourcing made easy
- How to scale this system to make as much money as you desire.